Deborah Hopkinson and YOU

Recent Titles in
The Author and YOU Series
Sharron L. McElmeel, Series Editor

Gerald McDermott and YOU
Jon C. Stott, Foreword and Illustrations by Gerald McDermott

Alma Flor Ada and YOU, Volume I
Alma Flor Ada

Jim Aylesworth and YOU
Jim Aylesworth and Jennifer K. Rotole

Toni Buzzeo and YOU
Toni Buzzeo

Jacqueline Briggs Martin and YOU
Jacqueline Briggs Martin with Sharron L. McElmeel

Bob Barner and YOU
Bob Barner

Mary Casanova and YOU
Mary Casanova

Jane Kurtz and YOU
Jane Kurtz

Deborah Hopkinson and YOU

Deborah Hopkinson

The Author and YOU

Sharron L. McElmeel, Series Editor

Westport, Connecticut • London

Library of Congress Cataloging-in-Publication Data

Hopkinson, Deborah.
　Deborah Hopkinson and you / Deborah Hopkinson.
　　p. cm. — (The author and you)
　Includes bibliographical references (p.　) and index.
　ISBN-13: 978-1-59158-278-6 (alk. paper)
　1. Hopkinson, Deborah. 2. Authors, American—20th century—Biography. 3. Children's literature—Authorship. I. Title.
PS3558.O6366Z46　　2007
828'.5409—dc22　　　2007013541
[B]

British Library Cataloguing in Publication Data is available.

Copyright © 2007 by Deborah Hopkinson

All rights reserved. No portion of this book may be
reproduced, by any process or technique, without the
express written consent of the publisher.

Library of Congress Catalog Card Number: 2007013541
ISBN-13: 978-1-59158-278-6

First published in 2007

Libraries Unlimited, 88 Post Road West, Westport, CT 06881
A Member of the Greenwood Publishing Group, Inc.
www.lu.com

Printed in the United States of America

The paper used in this book complies with the
Permanent Paper Standard issued by the National
Information Standards Organization (Z39.48–1984).

10　9　8　7　6　5　4　3　2　1

Cover Images

Cover of *Sky Boys: How They Built the Empire State Building* by Deborah Hopkinson. Jacket art © 2006 by James Ransome. Used by permission of Schwartz & Wade Books, an imprint of Random House, Inc.

Cover of *Sweet Land of Liberty* by Deborah Hopkinson. Jacket art © 2007 Leonard Jenkins. Used by permission of Peachtree Publishers.

Cover of *Sweet Clara and the Freedom Quilt* by Deborah Hopkinson. Jacket art © 1993 by James Ransome. Used by permission of Alfred A. Knopf, an imprint of Random House, Inc.

Cover of *Into the Firestorm: A Novel of San Francisco, 1906* by Deborah Hopkinson, reprinted by permission of Alfred A. Knopft, Inc., an imprint of Random House, Inc.

Contents

**Series Foreword by Sharon Coatney
  and Sharron L. McElmeel**   vii

Part I: So Many Stories to Tell: Meet Deborah Hopkinson   1

Chapter One: Nose in a Book   3
  An Ordinary Kid: A Brief Biography   4
  Becoming a Children's Writer   15

Chapter Two: History Must be Seen: Writing about the Past   17
  What Is Historical Fiction?   18
  So You Want to Write Historical Fiction . . .   19
  History Must Be Seen   23

Chapter Three: An Author's Process: Writing and Re-visioning   27
  Elements of Revision   28

Part II: So Many Worlds to Explore: Discover Deborah Hopkinson's Books   29

Chapter Four: The Underground Railroad and the Civil War   31
  Introduction   31
  Sweet Clara and the Freedom Quilt   31
  Under the Quilt of Night   33
  Billy and the Rebel   35
  From Slave to Soldier   37
  Making Connections   39
  Further Exploration   39

Chapter Five: Windows to the Past: Historical Fiction Picture Books   41
  Birdie's Lighthouse   41
  Maria's Comet   42
  A Band of Angels   44
  Fannie in the Kitchen   46
  Girl Wonder: A Baseball Story in Nine Innings   48
  Apples to Oregon   50
  Saving Strawberry Farm   52
  Sky Boys   53
  Sweet Land of Liberty   54

Making Connections　　55
Further Exploration　　55

Chapter Six: Young People in the Tumult of History: Longer Historical Fiction　　57
Introduction　　57
Kansas Before the Civil War: The Prairie Skies Series　　57
The Klondike Gold Rush: The Klondike Kid Series　　62
The Shirtwaist Strike and the Triangle Fire: *Dear America, Hear My Sorrow*　　67
The Great San Francisco Earthquake and Fire: *Into the Firestorm: A Novel of San Francisco, 1906*　　69
Making Connections　　70
Further Exploration　　71

Chapter Seven: Real People, Real Lives　　73
Introduction　　73
Life on the Lower East Side: *Shutting Out the Sky*　　73
Cotton in America: *Up Before Daybreak*　　75
Making Connections　　77
Further Exploration　　77

Chapter Eight: Bluebirds in the Garden: Two Picture Books Celebrating the Natural World　　79
Introduction　　79
Bluebird Summer　　79
A Packet of Seeds　　80
Making Connections　　81
Further Exploration　　82

Chapter Nine: Biographies of Memorable People　　83
Introduction　　83
John Adams　　83
Susan B. Anthony　　84
Charles Darwin　　86
Making Connections　　88
Further Exploration　　88

Appendices　　89

Bibliography　　91

Photo Credits　　95

Index　　99

Series Foreword

Have you ever wanted to sit down and talk with the author of a beloved story? Have you ever wanted to find out more? Good authors are like good friends. They touch our hearts and minds. They make us wonder and want to learn.

When young readers become engaged with story, they invariably ask questions.

- What comes first in Bob Barner's books, the words or the pictures? How does Bob Barner make his illustrations? Does he sing the songs he puts in his books?
- How long does it take Jim Aylesworth to write and retell his stories? Did he always know that he wanted to be a writer and poet?
- How does Jacqueline Briggs Martin find the inspiration for her stories? How does she research the facts for her stories?
- Is Jane Kurtz Ethiopian? Why does she write about Ethiopia? If she is from Ethiopia how come she knows so much about the Oregon Trail and Johnny Appleseed?
- And how does Deborah Hopkinson know about people like Fannie Farmer, Oscar Chapman, Henderson Luelling; where does she find out the information she needs to write a story?

As teachers and librarians, we know that the moment children begin asking questions, we are presented with a wonderful opportunity. In response, we may hold discussions or create learning activities. Yet, answers to some questions are hard to come by. After all, we and our students can't just sit down and talk with the authors we love and admire. But wouldn't it be great if we could?

Libraries Unlimited has developed *The Author and YOU* series to give you the next best thing to a real life visit with your favorite children's authors and illustrators. In these books, you'll hear from authors and illustrators as they reflect on their work and explain to YOU, the reader, what they really had in mind. You'll find answers to some of the questions you and your students might ask, and to some you never thought to ask.

Just as each author or illustrator is a unique individual, so will his or her conversation with YOU be unique and individual. There is no formula, no pre-designed structure. We've simply asked each author or illustrator to discuss the things they think are important or interesting about themselves and their books—and to share their comments with YOU.

Some authors will provide actual ideas and plans for you to use in sharing books with young readers. Others will share ideas that will help you generate your own ideas and connections to their work. In some cases the author writes the book in collaboration with another. In others, it is a private reflection; but in all cases you'll discover some fascinating information, and come away with valuable insights.

Previously this series has featured some notable authors and illustrators: Gerald McDermott, Alma Flor Ada, Toni Buzzeo, Jim Aylesworth, Jacqueline Briggs Martin, Mary Casanova, Jane Kurtz, and Bob Barner. This current addition to the series is authored by Deborah Hopkinson, who creates her stories with facts and information and a fast-moving, compelling narrative. We are excited to present Deborah Hopkinson's perspective on her life, research, and writing.

It is our hope that by giving you these special messages from authors and illustrators, *The Author and YOU* series will enhance your joy and understanding of literature—and in turn, will help YOU motivate young readers, surround them with literacy and literacy activities, and share the joy of understanding.

Sharon Coatney
Sharron McElmeel

PART I

So Many Stories to Tell: Meet Deborah Hopkinson

Chapter One
Nose in a Book

Whenever I see a kid with her head buried in a book, I see myself. From the time I was little, I loved to read more than just about anything else. And, to tell the truth, I haven't changed much over the years: if I'm at an airport engrossed in a good book, I'll sometimes walk right onto the plane still reading, oblivious to my surroundings.

That's one reason why whenever a young person asks for advice about becoming a writer, my answer is always the same: start by reading. Just as musicians listen to music throughout their lives, writers keep reading. And, like musicians, writers also constantly practice their craft. Being a writer is a lifelong commitment, an attempt with each story or book to do the best one can at that moment.

When I speak to students in schools, I try to convey that writing is difficult for just about all of us, and a lot of it comes down simply to

Autographing books during a school visit. (Dimitri Thomas)

practice and perseverance. I don't have magical abilities. It's also helpful, I think, for young people to know that writers started out just like them: ordinary kids. Authors aren't celebrities pursuing something unattainable, but regular people. Seeing it this way may help children understand that the dreams they may have—of becoming writers, artists, doctors, or just finishing college—are within their reach.

That's one reason why I like to show young people pictures of my everyday life: my family, my house, my pets, and both my jobs (although I am a writer I have a full-time job at Oregon State University). I also want my listeners to know that being a writer didn't happen overnight, like instant success or fame on a reality TV show. For me, as for most writers I know, getting published came about slowly, step by step, with a lot of dedication and determination along the way. And writing still requires a tremendous amount of time and hard work: ultimately that's what makes it so challenging and rewarding. I want kids and teachers to know that I still get rejection letters for stories and books, and, most importantly, I always, always revise everything I write.

Hard work is part of any career path. The essential thing is this: to realize your dreams, simply begin to take steps in the direction you want to go.

AN ORDINARY KID: A BRIEF BIOGRAPHY

I was born on February 4, 1952 in Lowell, Massachusetts, a city about thirty miles north of Boston. My parents, who are now deceased, were Russell and Gloria Hopkinson, who had also grown up in Massachusetts.

I was the oldest of three girls. My sister, Bonnie, is about three years younger, and my sister, Janice, is five years my junior. We are all close and in regular contact, although we're spread across the country. I try to see my sisters and my nieces, Jamie, Kelly, and Haley, whenever possible.

Although my parents were not able to go to college, they always believed that we could, and they gave my sisters and me their full support. I was the first person in our family to graduate from college, thanks to part-time jobs and scholarships—and the encouragement I got from my family and teachers.

If you ask my two younger sisters what they remember most about me from our childhood, I am sure they would say, "Deborah always had her nose in a book! And she stayed up all night reading."

We did have time, though, to roam the neighborhood and play in the back yard; we loved the swing set my dad set up for us. My dad was an avid trout fisherman, and for many summers my parents vacationed

Nose in a Book 5

My parents on their honeymoon.

My parents and me: Authors were once babies, too!

Me at one year: Not reading just yet!

A big snowstorm when I was two.

Rebekah Hopkinson in Maine.

in the northwest corner of Maine, in a small town called Rangeley, where my father would take a canoe onto tranquil Quimby Pond in the early mornings. After my mother's death in 1985, my father continued the tradition, accompanied by a dear friend, Kathleen Clark.

Like my dad, I fell in love with Maine. After college I spent one summer in Rangeley as a waitress at a backwoods lodge, and at the end of the season my friend and I hiked a hundred miles of the Appalachian Trail together. Over the years, I tried to time my visits back home to coincide with the annual Rangeley vacation, and my daughter, Rebekah, can still remember picking Maine blueberries when she was little.

Although our family lived frugally and didn't have a lot of extra money, my parents always did what they could to support our activities. One event I remember is the annual bicycle and doll carriage parade when I was in kindergarten. Thanks to my parents' help with decorating, I won a prize with my doll carriage. Of course, looking back, this whole notion seems very dated, but I wasn't quite ready at the age of five to ask: "Why do I have to push a doll carriage? Can't I ride my bike, too?"

As I've mentioned, reading was a big part of my childhood, but I don't recall having many picture books except for a special few: I still own a copy of *Make Way for Ducklings* which my grandmother gave to me on my second birthday.

I do have vivid memories of curling up with longer books. Early favorites were *The Secret Garden* and *The Little Princess* by Frances Hodgson Burnett. I devoured series like the Trixie Beldon books and the *Happy Hollisters*. And I still remember waking one Christmas morning to find a whole box of books with my name on it under the tree.

Not only did I stay up late into the night reading, especially during school vacations and the summer, I was also known to read at school—and not just during reading time. I just couldn't bear to stop in the middle of a chapter, so I'd prop up whatever book I was reading behind a big history or geography textbook in class. (I don't think I ever got caught!)

While I read a lot of fiction, I developed an early interest in history. In those days, there weren't as many high-quality nonfiction works or biographies being written for young people as there are now. But I recall one series I've always referred to as "the orange biographies." I read about the lives of Clara Barton and Jesse Fremont, but most of the books were about presidents and generals: men. I can remember wondering why there weren't more books about women in history.

I was also intrigued by the stories behind the facts and dates in my textbooks. Once, in our fourth-grade history book, I came across a paragraph about the Underground Railroad. That paragraph seemed so short. I can remember sitting at my desk thinking, "There just has to be more!" Like many kids, I wasn't drawn to memorizing facts, the dates of past wars, or the names of presidents. I was interested in the people. What sparked my interest most were the profiles and the stories in the "shaded boxes" of the history textbook.

As I look back, I think one reason I read so much was that I wasn't very good at team sports, like kickball or softball. I've always been short, even in elementary school. I didn't fit in well with the most popular kids. And I was sometimes teased for being an all-A student—the kid who always seemed to win the spelling bee.

I suppose you could say reading was partly a way of escaping the social pressures of school. But it also set me on a lifelong path. I have no recollection of the moment when I first decided I wanted to be a writer. But I do have a copy of a short newspaper bio of me in sixth grade, when I was chosen to represent my elementary school in the city spelling bee. My bio says that I wanted to be a doctor or a writer. It would be years before I actually set about writing in a serious way, but the early desire was there.

Reading helped me find a world I loved. I might not fit in at recess, but somehow I belonged in the world of books, ideas, stories, and imagination—if only I could find a way to get there.

A winning doll carriage!

In 1966, I entered Lowell High School as a sophomore. I continued to read fiction of all kinds throughout high school, and especially loved historical fiction and British literature. I was fortunate enough to take Advanced Placement English. I had always liked doing research. I'd written some long term papers, which my mother had typed for me. (The ones I remember are papers on the history of horse racing in the United States and a long paper on Sacajawea.) Now we were being asked to write complex essays in class, and I remember being pleased when my teacher complimented me on one, noting that it had "the usual Hopkinson style." I'd certainly never even realized I had a style!

Although I graduated among the top in my class, money for college was limited, but I did get a few scholarships. So in 1969, at age 17,

My elementary school in Lowell, Massachusetts.

On a visit back home in front of Lowell High School. (Dimitri Thomas)

I moved to Amherst, Massachusetts, to enter the University of Massachusetts at Amherst as an English major—with my best friend, Vicki Hemphill, as my roommate. We lived on the fourth floor of a high-rise dorm, quite a change for two rather naïve and inexperienced girls. It was a turbulent time to be on a college campus, and in my freshman year I participated in a student strike to protest the Vietnam War.

The University of Massachusetts was about eighty miles from home, and so going to college became my first experience away from my parents and my sisters. But, maybe because I had always read about adventures, I was restless for some of my own. I couldn't afford to go to a college out of state, but in my sophomore year, I entered a domestic exchange program at the University of Hawai'i at Manoa, in Honolulu. This was a marvelous opportunity that allowed students to attend an out-of-state college for a year, for the same tuition costs as their home school.

I had been on one airplane trip in my life—and now I was flying thousands of miles away. Stepping off the plane in Honolulu, I can still remember how magical everything looked and smelled: the air was perfumed with plumeria blossoms, the ocean sparkled, and the hills of O'ahu boasted deep, luscious plants and trees I'd never imagined back East.

That year in Honolulu was life-changing in many ways. I took my one and only creative writing class. I also found that I felt very much at home in Hawaii's diverse cultures and physical beauty, perhaps more at home than I'd ever felt in Lowell.

As a matter of fact, I fell so much in love with Hawaii that although I did go back to finish my degree in Massachusetts, I returned a few years later to the University of Hawai'i for a master's degree in Asian Studies, which I completed in 1978. And then I stayed—for nearly 20 years. In graduate school I also met my husband, Andy Thomas.

By 1978, I had two degrees—but, unfortunately, no job prospects. I found my first professional position as a staff writer for the American Red Cross in Honolulu. This was the start of a career for nonprofit organizations and higher education institutions in grant writing and fundraising (also called development or advancement) which I've always pursued simultaneously with writing.

Like many people I know, I didn't know anything about the field of development before I fell into my first job. But I have found working in philanthropy an exciting and rewarding career. From the American Red Cross, I took a job at a community theatre, and then a K–12 private school. I then began working in higher education, raising funds primarily from private foundations for the University of Hawai'i and the East-West Center in Honolulu; Whitman College in Walla Walla, Washington; and, my present position as director of

Andy Thomas and Deborah Hopkinson. (Dimitri Thomas)

foundation relations at Oregon State University Foundation in Corvallis, Oregon.

While it's not easy to find time to write, I know I am very lucky to have a challenging and demanding profession. Every day, I work with world-class scientists and educators on some of the major issues of our time, including climate change, water and watersheds, medical research, and K–12 science and math education.

My husband, Andy Thomas, is now an assistant winemaker in Oregon, but he began as an art student. We have two children. Rebekah, born in 1984, and Dimitri, who was born in Russia in 1986 and came to our family in 1992, when he was six. Our rented house in Honolulu was very small, and with housing so expensive we decided to move back to the mainland after we adopted Dimitri. So in 1994, we left Honolulu and moved to Walla Walla, Washington, where I took a job in the development office of Whitman College, a small, private liberal arts college. We were able to buy a house for the first time, and our large yard gave us the chance to garden and have pets.

Nose in a Book **13**

My son, Dimitri, with his dog, Kona. (Deborah Hopkinson)

My daughter, Rebekah, and husband, Andy. (Deborah Hopkinson)

Dimitri and our dog, Pea (pronounced "pay-uh," it's the transliteration of the word "bear" in Hawaiian). (Deborah Hopkinson)

Sharing the joy of books with my children has been a wonderful experience. When Dimitri was in elementary and middle school, he sometimes accompanied me to school visits. Since my presentation also included slides of my family, especially his many pets, we often found that students wanted his autograph even more than mine! And they loved to ask questions about the latest additions to his menagerie, which over the years has included chinchillas, ferrets, roosters, quail, geese, chickens, frogs, pigeons, turkeys, peacocks, and sheep!

BECOMING A CHILDREN'S WRITER

Although I'd wanted to be a writer for a long time, except for keeping a diary, taking one class, and trying my hand at a few stories, I'd actually never *done* much creative writing. By the time Rebekah was born in 1984, most of my writing was taking place at work. By then I was a successful grant proposal writer, raising funds for research and programs at the University of Hawai'i.

Yet my long-held desire to write books didn't go away. Just before Rebekah was born, I'd experienced the severe pain of a kidney stone: a somber reminder, that, although I was a healthy young woman, life was short. If I wanted to be a published author, I had better start somewhere. Otherwise, it would be a lost, unfulfilled dream. But how could I write, work, and still take care of my young daughter? Tackling a 300-page adult novel just seemed overwhelming.

But as Rebekah and I visited the library each week to check out picture books, an idea occurred to me. I'd always imagined myself as a novelist. But what about starting with picture books? They were certainly short—short enough for a working mother to write at night after my little girl was in bed, or early on a weekend morning.

And so when Rebekah was about three years old I began writing and submitting stories to publishers. But all I got for about two years were rejections. Then I had the chance to attend a workshop organized by the Society of Children's Book Writers and Illustrators, a professional organization for writers and illustrators of children's literature. At this workshop, the presenter suggested that new authors try getting published in magazines first to develop a track record—and then tackle book publishers.

And so I began sending my stories to children's magazines and finally, in January 1990, *Cricket* magazine published my first story, titled "Skate, Kirsten, Skate." (I still recommend magazines for new writers, and student writers can also find writing contests to enter.) Over the years I have continued to publish fiction and nonfiction in magazines, both in *Cricket* as well as Scholastic's *Storyworks*.

I also published a nonfiction book for the school and library market on Pearl Harbor, but it was never available in a bookstore, so I didn't quite feel like a real writer—yet. Then, in 1989 I wrote a story titled, *Sweet Clara and the Freedom Quilt.* I based the story on a piece about African American quilts that I heard on National Public Radio. I sent the story to several publishers who all rejected it. In October 1990 I sent the story out again, and the next month I received a phone call at work. I will always remember that moment—and the excitement of that life-changing day. I picked up the phone and a voice said, "My name is Anne Schwartz; I'm an editor at Random House. We'd like to publish your book."

Since then I have sold more than thirty books, many of which are described in the following chapters. I continue to work full-time, balancing writing and my job.

My future titles include picture books on ethnomusicologist John Lomax and explorer Matthew Henson, a tall tale inspired by the first girl to deliver the mail in a California stagecoach, a picture book about Charles Darwin's family, and a story from Abraham Lincoln's childhood. I hope also to complete another middle-grade novel and more nonfiction. I feel fortunate to be part of the world of children's literature, and love sharing my work with children, teachers, librarians, and parents.

Chapter Two
History Must be Seen: Writing about the Past

When I was first trying to get published, I didn't write about history. Instead, my early efforts included stories about talking vegetables, mice, and crickets. There was even one about a chicken that stowed away in a passenger train. While there's nothing wrong with talking crickets or train-riding chickens, the truth is that most of my first stories simply weren't very good.

One piece of advice that new writers usually get is, "Write what you know." I don't think this means that you only have to write about things that have actually happened to you. Rather, for me this piece of advice has meant trying to write as authentically as possible. And I find that I do this best when I write about issues and topics I care about passionately.

I began writing about the past from a simple desire: to find out more about the lives of ordinary people in history, especially girls and women. The history books I read in school seemed to be full of men:

Working at the computer, with our cat, Sophie, in the way! (Dimitri Thomas)

generals, kings, and presidents. There just weren't many women in those books. And even though I liked true-life adventures such as Sir Edmund Hilary's assault on Mt. Everest, or long historical fiction novels by authors like James Michener and Kenneth Roberts, I always felt something was missing.

Historical fiction and high-quality nonfiction works have come into their own in the past ten or twenty years. These books, which include many about previously unrecognized women, have replaced the limited biographies that were available when I was a child. And just as adults have been captivated by such bestsellers as *Seabiscuit*, kids now can read about a wide range of heroes and heroines in sports, science, exploration, and politics. These stories can help all of us develop a more nuanced and complex understanding of historical time periods and events.

WHAT IS HISTORICAL FICTION?

I like to read—and write—both historical fiction and nonfiction. But they're not the same. Good historical fiction can help readers of all ages imagine the past, but it's no substitute for the actual study of history through primary sources and outstanding informational works. It's especially important that young readers understand just how different historical fiction is in purpose and scope from nonfiction.

The key word in the term "historical fiction" is fiction. While historical fiction can help expand interest in a time period or bring otherwise dry events to life, it is first and foremost "a made-up story." Once writers invent dialogue, scenes, or characters, and embellish the facts, the work is clearly fiction—no matter how closely the events or characters follow actual historical occurrences. As I often tell students, as soon as I put words into the mouth of a historical person, I'm creating fiction.

That's not to say that historical fiction can't help breathe life into history. I think historical fiction can serve as a jumping-off point to learn more about a certain event or time period, or help sow the seeds of a lifelong love of history in young readers. When I write historical fiction, I aim to inspire readers to dig further and say, "Now I want to find out more about what really happened." The best historical fiction helps readers imagine themselves in another time and place. It should spark critical thinking as well as emotional connections.

SO YOU WANT TO WRITE HISTORICAL FICTION...

Finding Story Ideas

When I visit schools, students always want to know where I get my ideas. I usually lob the question back, "Well, I'm no different from you. Where do you get *your ideas*?"

In fact, story ideas are all around us: in newspapers, radio, books, museums, roadside markers, the Internet, library and museum exhibits, and of course, in our personal experiences. My picture book, *Maria's Comet*, grew out of finding Maria Mitchell's name on an Internet calendar of famous women; *Fannie in the Kitchen* evolved after reading about the real Fannie Farmer in an anthology of women inventors.

In searching for story ideas, I also try to pay attention to what topics are being covered in the classroom. Since my first picture book was published in 1993, I've come to appreciate the role educators and librarians play as proponents and caretakers of our literary heritage. Teachers and librarians help to keep many historical fiction books alive. They also use books across the curriculum. For example, *Sweet Clara and the Freedom Quilt* has been incorporated into social studies units as well as in mathematics activities.

My son, Dimitri—when he was younger, during a research trip to a living history museum. (Deborah Hopkinson)

What Makes a Good Story Idea

As I've become more aware of the creative ways my books are used in classrooms, I've been careful to include historical notes and background information. For example, *Girl Wonder* includes a timeline of women in baseball. *Maria's Comet* includes both a historical note on Maria Mitchell, as well as a glossary of astronomy definitions. *A Band of*

Jubilee Singers exhibit at Fisk University Library, Nashville, TN. (Deborah Hopkinson)

Angels includes a historical note and, on the endpapers, biographical information on the original Jubilee singers whose stories inspired the book.

Do you like to read about things that happened a long time ago? Would you like to write a story set in the past? Suppose you hear about something on the radio, or read a newspaper article about something that happened in the past that makes you curious to learn more. Maybe it's a big storm that folks still talk about year later, a family story about a long-lost aunt who saved her cat from drowning, or someone who accomplished something unusual.

But how do you know which of these ideas will make good stories? Here are some questions to ask when you first come across an idea that grabs your attention:

- Do the elements of a good story exist in the material? In other words, is there the potential for conflict? Do the characters' lives have the power to engage the reader?
- If you want to write for young readers, it is usually helpful to have a child in the story. Are there any children in the story you have found? If not, is it possible to tell the story from a child's point of view?

- How about the subject of the story? Will it be interesting to your readers, especially if they are kids?
- What about pictures? If you want to write a picture book for young readers, will the story lend itself to being illustrated?
- Is this a story that in your heart you feel *needs* to be told? And do you feel you are the right person to take it on?

Research

I love doing research. To me, there's nothing more exciting than stepping onto a university campus and walking into a research library. And, of course, the Internet has made finding information a lot faster and easier. But while the Internet has made the research process easier, it has also brought challenges. Information literacy—knowing how to find, evaluate, use, and communicate information well—is more important than ever for students and for writers.

For me, research usually begins when I encounter a story that grabs me and piques my curiosity. When I first read about Jubilee singer Ella Sheppard and astronomer Maria Mitchell I wanted to find out more. The more I learned, the more I felt connected to these amazing human beings; I could almost feel the vibrancy of their remarkable spirits across time. After I learned as much as I could, I then tried to craft stories to share that connection.

In the research process, it's helpful to consult with experts and others who may know about your story. For example, I was fortunate that Beth Howse, a descendent of Ella Sheppard and a librarian at Fisk, was willing to read the manuscript of *A Band of Angels* in draft form. Still, errors can happen, and the best you can do is to keep scrupulous notes, take responsibility for accuracy, and, of course, "Check your work!"

I probably learned most of my research skills as an undergraduate and graduate student. But the research I've done as a writer far exceeds anything I attempted in school. Here are some tips:

- Gather as many secondary and primary sources on your topic as possible. Learn how to evaluate both. For instance, a book written for general knowledge without footnotes will often be less helpful than a footnoted secondary source from an academic press that represents years of research from a scholar's dissertation.
- Evaluate the source. Newspapers are often good sources, but they can be inaccurate or biased. Look at the biographies, source notes, bibliographies, and other works by the same author of a secondary source.

- Get your work reviewed by several reliable sources. For my nonfiction works I relied on scholars in the field. In one case, a professor introduced me to a young researcher who had written an unpublished journal article on my topic based on new information that helped me better understand the topic.
- Don't be afraid to pick up the phone or e-mail experts. Most academics or experts are helpful, and will answer questions or recommend books to you.
- If possible, do research in person. Going there and seeing a place you are writing about with your own eyes is invaluable.

Exhibit on baseball pioneer Alta Weiss at the Norwalk Public Library, in Norwalk, OH. (Deborah Hopkinson)

Writing the Story

Let's say your idea has all the elements of a good story, you've done your research, and you're ready to write. Where to start? I wish I had one of Fannie Farmer's foolproof recipes to offer, but when I look at my own books and how they came to be, about the only thing I can tell you for sure is to keep trying—and never throw away research or a story idea.

Sometimes the biggest challenge is finding the right voice for a story. In my first draft of *A Band of Angels*, I told the story from Ella Sheppard's point of view, relating her experiences as one of the founding members of the Jubilee Singers of Fisk University. But my editor felt that it wasn't child-centered enough, and it took several more revisions to create the story-within-a-story format of the final book.

One of the biggest challenges in writing historical fiction is deciding what and how much of your research to include. I usually end up with much more material than I can ever use. Often I find that my first drafts are boring, and lack a strong dramatic arc: I hate to give up those little details I uncovered during the research process. I usually have to revise and sometimes fictionalize to make the story more compelling for young readers, another reason why historical fiction should never be used in place of a good informational book.

Other times the challenge is finding the right format for your material. Years ago I wrote an (unpublished) Civil War novel. In the course of researching it, I came across a true story of a deserter in the battle of Gettysburg. When it seemed clear the novel was destined to find a permanent home in my closet, I tried re-working the deserter incident into a picture book. That wasn't right either. But when I had the opportunity to write easy readers, I pulled out my research once more, and the result was *Billy and the Rebel*. So, never throw that research away.

Sometimes a story simply isn't strong enough for an entire book. Magazines offer wonderful opportunities for working with editors, compiling a track record, and reaching young readers. If you have a historical fiction idea, creating a short magazine piece might be the perfect way to share your story.

HISTORY MUST BE SEEN

History isn't just an endless series of dates and battles to memorize. The past is full of stories of real lives, the lives of our parents and grandparents and great-grandparents reaching further and further back into time. Without stories about the past, it can be easy to forget the events that have shaped the present.

Through historical fiction and nonfiction, we can begin to tune our ears to listen for those echoes of the past that come down to us through time. Stories help us empathize and become connected to one another. To study the past is to search for truth and meaning, not just in the lives of others, but in our own lives. After reading *Birdie's Lighthouse*, my picture book inspired by a nineteenth-century lighthouse keeper, one young girl wrote me, "I have a connection to Birdie because when my dad left I had to raise money. I learned that if you work hard enough you can do anything."

When I speak to school groups, I always ask kids what kinds of books they like to read. Historical fiction is hardly ever mentioned:

Jubilee Hall at Fisk University, Nashville, TN. (Deborah Hopkinson)

scary stories, animal stories, fantasy, and mysteries rank far higher. My job is to create excitement! I show photographs of people I've met, places I've visited, even the listening equipment used to hear oral history interviews. I describe how Ella Shepherd and the Jubilee Singers gave concerts all over the world to raise money for their school, now Fisk University. Then I show a photograph of Jubilee Hall, which the singers made possible.

This photograph always elicits gasps of amazement. It's partly, I think, because the building itself is so beautiful. Its very presence helps students to understand, "This was real. It happened. These people lived and breathed."

By the end of my presentation, kids can't wait to touch the replica of Sweet Clara's quilt, pointing out the path she took on the Underground Railroad.

Jubilee Hall historical marker at Fisk University, Nashville, TN. (Deborah Hopkinson)

Doing research in Kansas for the Prairie Skies Series. (Michele Hill)

Writing has brought me back to history, to the search for all those missing people and stories I wanted to know about when I was in fourth grade. And sometimes what I find is so astonishing I feel the need to share it.

I find it harder, though, to speak in public about how encounters with the past actually make me feel. How I get chills when I walk up the worn steps of Jubilee Hall; how the spirit of another person seems to reach across time through their words and touch mine; or how people seem to stare out of photographs and dare me to come stand beside them. It's hard for me to speak about how, when the research is done and I'm ready to write, I often just close my eyes and "go there."

In the nineteenth century, pioneering history educator Lucy Maynard Salmon said, "History must be seen." Discovering stories that have the power to inspire is one of the joys I take in reading—and writing—about the past.

Chapter Three
An Author's Process: Writing and Re-visioning

Perseverance and determination are perhaps the most crucial things a writer needs. But a close third is the ability and willingness to revise.

I've been able to take a lot of what I've learned from my fund-raising career and apply it to my writing. Being responsible for many grant proposals has taught me that writing is almost always collaborative. I may be the one to draft a proposal, but it's likely to be critiqued by lots of "editors": professors, researchers, deans, colleagues, and vice presidents. Revising based on others' comments in this way has become second nature. I've learned to trust that this process almost always produces a better final product than I could by working alone.

For this reason, I focus quite a bit on revision when I present to students. I talk about the editorial process and then ask them to identify *their* editors: teachers, parents, maybe even a friend or sibling. I want young writers to know that not only is it okay for others to comment on and ask them to change their writing, but that this, in fact, is how most writing works in the real world.

I also dig into the word revision itself. I remind students that when we get our vision tested, we're checking our eyes. And so the word "revision" actually means to "see again." In other words, when we do additional drafts or "sloppy copies" of a piece of writing, we're not just correcting spelling or making it neater. The process of revision is to try to look at our writing with new eyes, as though we have never seen it before. In this way, we can create the best and most effective story, grant proposal, or school report we can.

Some years ago I learned another important aspect of revision through my job—the hard way. I was in charge of a large public event. I was required to write the speeches, including an address from the university president, who was presenting teaching awards to faculty.

But although I had proofread the information for every person getting an award, I neglected one important step. As the president was making the awards, recognizing each person in alphabetical order, there was a stir from one table. Someone had been forgotten! In other words, I had proofread and revised what was there—but not what wasn't there. Looking at what might be missing from a piece of writing is an essential part of revising.

Revision takes time. What you see one day is different from what you see the next. Stories, like bread dough, seem to come alive as they sit. New ideas, connections, and possibilities appear. And then, somehow, it feels done.

ELEMENTS OF REVISION

Point of View and Voice

Novels such as *Speak* or *Out of the Dust* are memorable because of the first-person narrator's compelling, distinctive voice. Just as in a novel, voice is important in a picture book for older children. It's not easy to find the right voice or point of view. Try several "ways in" to your story, and don't be afraid to make drastic changes. As noted earlier, in my first draft of *A Band of Angels*, I told the story from Ella Sheppard's point of view. My editor didn't feel it was child-centered enough. Eventually I tried a story-within-a-story format, with both a child narrator and the story told by her aunt.

Plot and Setting

Plot is the skeleton, the framework of beginning, middle, and end, and the momentum that moves the story forward. In a picture book, plot is more abbreviated than in a novel, and usually there isn't room for subplots. There are many good reference books available on the mechanics of writing. For the basics, I prefer Robert McKee's *Story*.

Characterization

Characterization is one of the most powerful aspects of a story. As much as possible, I try to make use of the same multidimensional character elements in a picture book as a longer work of fiction. Characters change in the course of the story as they confront challenges and problems. A character must be credible, and the reader must believe that the character could do what she or he does.

For me, writing is rewarding because it presents so many challenges. Every time I tackle a new project, I learn something new. Maybe it's a bit like mountaineers: it's not those few moments on the summit that mean the most. The satisfaction comes from taking on a difficult, complicated challenge—and living to tell the tale.

PART II

So Many Worlds to Explore: Discover Deborah Hopkinson's Books

Chapter Four
The Underground Railroad and the Civil War

INTRODUCTION

In Part Two, I'd like to share a little bit about the books I've written. Each chapter in this section is arranged thematically and focuses on several titles. I've also included short bibliographies for further reading. The changing nature of Internet sites makes it impractical to include Web sites, but my homepage, www.deborahhopkinson.com, includes links to Web sites, classroom activities, and lesson plans. A complete bibliography of published works as well as major awards is included in Part Three.

The four works in this chapter are historical fiction stories about the Underground Railroad and the Civil War. Two are picture books illustrated by James Ransome, based on folklore surrounding quilts and the Underground Railroad. The other two are early readers inspired by the experiences of actual people who lived through the Civil War.

SWEET CLARA AND THE FREEDOM QUILT

Sweet Clara and the Freedom Quilt. Illustrated by James Ransome. Alfred A. Knopf, 1993.

> *We went north, following the trail of the freedom quilt. All the things people told me about, all the tiny stitches I took, now I could see real things. There was the old tree struck down by lightning, the winding road near the creek, the hunting path through the swamp. It was like being in a dream you already dreamed.*

The inspiration for *Sweet Clara and the Freedom Quilt* came one morning in June 1989, when I heard a story on National Public Radio about an exhibition of African American quilts at Williams College. Most quilt historians discount the notion that quilts with maps and secret codes were part of the Underground Railroad, although folklore and oral traditions linking the two persist. And so it is important that readers understand that this story and *Under the Quilt of Night* are fiction.

In this book, Clara is a young girl who has been sent away from her mother to work on another plantation. Befriended by a woman she

Sweet Clara and the Freedom Quilt Cover

calls Aunt Rachel, Clara learns to sew and becomes a seamstress in the Big House, where she hears about the Underground Railroad and is determined to try to escape. One impediment, of course, is the lack of a map to show the way, as well as the ability to read, since Clara has never been allowed to go to school. To overcome these obstacles, Sweet Clara decides to sew a quilt containing the information she needs.

Clara gathers information for her map from the people in her community. When it is done, she and a young friend escape, leaving the quilt behind. James Ransome's luminous oil paintings capture Clara's determined spirit and help readers imagine the quilt she creates.

UNDER THE QUILT OF NIGHT

Under the Quilt of Night. Illustrated by James E. Ransome. Atheneum Books for Young Readers, 2002.

*Now he wants to track me, catch me
chase me till my breath is gone,
fence me in to be a slave again.
But I'll make my steps
quick whispers in the dark.
I'll run where he won't find me.
under the quilt of night.*

Under the Quilt of Night is an imagined journey made by an unnamed family along the Underground Railroad. It was inspired by one of the

Under the Quilt of Night Cover

Illustration from *Under the Quilt of Night*, page 3

prevailing myths surrounding the Underground Railroad conductors: that quilts with dark centers were used to mark safe houses for escaping slaves. The book was written in 1997, shortly after James Ransome and I met for the first time. Rather than a sequel to *Sweet Clara and the Freedom Quilt*, this book is meant to be a companion title, showing another aspect of the Underground Railroad. Once again, while some of the details, such as slaves hiding in compartments in wagons are based on fact, *Under the Quilt of Night* is fiction.

Like the story's narrator, most of the names of those who managed to escape slavery are lost to history. We do know that escape was extremely difficult, if not impossible, for most enslaved people. James Ransome's palate of deep blues and purples underscores the tension and danger of such a journey.

BILLY AND THE REBEL

Billy and the Rebel. Illustrated by Brian Floca. Atheneum Books for Young Readers, 2005.

> *It wasn't Papa after all. Instead it was a boy.*
> *In the candlelight, Billy could see that he wore a dirty, gray uniform. This boy was a Confederate soldier.*

Most writers have a pile of projects that end up in the back of the closet. Years ago, I drafted a manuscript about the battle of Gettysburg. Although the novel was never published, I kept my research notes,

Billy and the Rebel Cover

Illustration from *Billy and the Rebel*, page 17

which included information about William Bayly, a young boy whose family took in a Confederate deserter during the July 1863 battle.

Billy and the Rebel, a Level 3 Ready-to-Read, is based on William Bayly's memories of the battle, written in 1903, 40 years after the event. William Bayly remembered how the young Rebel helped him break off branches of cherry trees to feed the Rebel soldiers. Confronted by a Confederate soldier, the 13-year-old Billy was pulled back by his deserter friend. William Bayly's mother, Harriet, who also wrote of the incident, recalled that the deserter remained in the area after the war, where he married and settled down. The Adams County Historical Society in Pennsylvania sent me the Bayly memoirs, but I could not trace the name of the deserter, so he is known simply as "Cousin" in this story of an unlikely friendship.

FROM SLAVE TO SOLDIER

From Slave to Soldier. Illustrated by Brian Floca. Atheneum Books for Young Readers, 2005.

Well, since it's not your farm and not your mule, why don't you come along with us? We could use a strong boy like you. You can join the Union army and be free.

One of my favorite things about libraries is discovering new books. Call number in hand, I may be searching for one specific book—but

From Slave to Soldier Cover

Illustration by Brian Floca from *From Slave to Soldier*, page 27

then find myself leaving the library with an armful of titles from nearby shelves.

And that is exactly how I found out about John McCline. McCline was a former slave and Civil War veteran whose memoir was edited by Jan Furman and published in 1998 as part of the Voices of the Civil War Series of the University of Tennessee Press as *Slavery in the Clover Bottoms: John McCline's Narrative of His Life during Slavery and the Civil War*.

A Level 3 Ready-to-Read, *From Slave to Soldier* is the fictionalized story of how eleven-year-old John McCline walked off a Tennessee plantation one day to join a group of Union soldiers with the Thirteenth

Michigan Infantry Regiment. Young John became a mule team driver's helper during the war.

Unlike many African Americans who were treated poorly during the Civil War, John was, in fact, befriended by several men in the regiment. They assisted him both during and after the war. John McCline eventually landed in Santa Fe, New Mexico, where, around 1930, he showed a handwritten version of his memoir to his employer. McCline married at age 86 and died in 1948, at about age 95. Although it was not published during his lifetime, the manuscript survived. With its vivid depiction of plantation life and detailed descriptions of life in the Union army, *Slavery in the Clover Bottoms* reminds us of the richness and diversity of individual experience.

MAKING CONNECTIONS

The books in this section might be used in conjunction with further reading or activities related to:

- Research on the Underground Railroad, either locally or nationally;
- Quilt projects using paper in the classroom;
- Research community and regional quilts;
- Slavery and the causes of the Civil War;
- Black soldiers in the Civil War.

FURTHER EXPLORATION

Hamilton, Virginia. *Many Thousand Gone: African Americans from Slavery to Freedom.* Illustrated by Leo and Diane Dillon. Knopf, 1993.
Levine, Ellen. Illustrated by Larry Williams. *If You Traveled on the Underground Railroad.* Scholastic, 1992.
Lyons, Mary E. *Letters from a Slave Girl: The Story of Harriet Jacobs.* Scribner & Maxwell Macmillan International, 1992.
Paulsen, Gary. *Nightjohn.* Delacorte Press, 1993.
Polacco, Patricia. *The Keeping Quilt.* Simon & Schuster Books for Young Readers, 1988.
Ringgold, Faith. *Aunt Harriet's Undergrond Railroad in the Sky.* Crown, 1992.
Schroeder, Alan., Illustrated by Jerry Pinkney. *Minty: A Story of Young Harriet Tubman.* Dial Books for Young Readers, 1996.
Weatherford, Carol Boston. *Moses: When Harriet Tubman Led Her People to Freedom.* Illustrated by Kadir Nelson. Hyperion Books for Children, 2006.
Winter, Jeanette. *Follow the Drinking Gourd.* Knopf, 1988.

Chapter Five
Windows to the Past: Historical Fiction Picture Books

Many of my picture books are historical fiction, small windows that allow us glimpses of the past. I'm particularly fascinated by little-known stories of women in history, and am delighted that my books may help to bring these tales to new readers. While some of the historical fiction books in this section are based very closely on the lives of real people, others represent flights of the imagination. History can be serious, but it can also be fun.

BIRDIE'S LIGHTHOUSE

Birdie's Lighthouse. Illustrated by Kimberly Bulcken Root. Atheneum Books for Young Readers, 1997.

Birdie's Lighthouse Cover

Soon the lantern room glowed, and the beam reached out into the darkness like a bright strand of hope.

Birdie's Lighthouse is the diary of Birdie Holland's tenth year, in 1855, when she and her family move from their small Maine fishing village to Turtle Island, where her father has been named the light keeper. The story was inspired by the life of nineteenth-century Maine lighthouse keeper Abigail Burgess Grant, who began helping her father keep the lights on Matinicus Rock when she was a girl.

Life on the bleak island isn't easy. Birdie's diary records her feelings as she struggles to adjust to her new world. The daughter of a former seaman, Birdie knows the danger and power of the ocean. She watches the clouds carefully to predict an upcoming storm and in its midst whispers to the ocean, "Please don't be so angry."

After Birdie's brother, Nate, leaves to go work on a fishing boat, Birdie takes on his role of helping her father. Slowly, as she takes on more responsibility for the lamps, Birdie comes to love the lighthouse and Turtle Island. When her father is ill, Birdie braves a fierce storm to get to the lighthouse tower to check the lights. Like the real-life Abigail Burgess Grant, by the close of the story Birdie comes to feel that the light has become a part of her.

MARIA'S COMET

Maria's Comet. Illustrated by Deborah Lanino. Atheneum Books for Young Readers, 1999.

Maria's Comet Cover

*Someday, Papa says, we'll know what comets are made of,
But for now they are mysterious visitors,
With blurry heads and glowing tails
Like ancient creatures gliding through the deep.*

The real Maria (pronounced Mariah) Mitchell was born on August 1, 1818, in Nantucket, Massachusetts, into a large Quaker family. Maria inherited her father's passion for astronomy. As a young woman, she worked as a librarian in the Nantucket Atheneum by day, and pursued her astronomy studies at night. Maria's life of obscurity ended when she received international recognition after her discovery of a telescopic comet on October 1, 1847. In 1848 she became the first woman member of the American Academy of Arts and Sciences. By 1865 she had been recruited by Matthew Vassar to become professor of astronomy and directory of the observatory at his new college for women.

Maria Mitchell dreamed of being a scientist at a time when most women did not work outside the home. She desired to explore, to discover. An association bearing her name is active today, along with an observatory and professorship in her honor at Vassar College.

Just as impressive as Maria Mitchell's record of scientific achievement are her progressive ideas on women's education. As a child, Maria spent a lot of time doing what other young girls did: sewing, mending, and performing necessary household chores. What made Maria extraordinary was the support of her parents for girls' education, along with her burning desire and passion for knowledge, and her commitment to long hours of study and observation with her telescope.

Maria's Comet is a fictionalized account of Maria's desire to study astronomy as a young child. The book includes an author's note as well as a glossary of astronomical terms.

A Band of Angels Cover

A BAND OF ANGELS

A Band of Angels. Illustrated by Raul Colon. Atheneum Books for Young Readers, 2001.

> *Sometimes songs arise from happiness, sometimes from sorrow. When Ella heard the news about her school, her heart was so heavy she just had to sing.*

Ella Sheppard Moore was born on February 4, 1851, in Nashville, Tennessee. Left penniless when her father died, Ella made her way to Fisk School, a school for former slaves. She joined the school's chorus

Windows to the Past: Historical Fiction Picture Books **45**

Illustration from *A Band of Angels*, page 25. Ella at the piano with other Jubilee Singers

and did odd jobs to stay in school. Ella became one of the original Jubilee Singers, whose concert tours in the 1870s introduced spirituals to the world and raised about $150,000, enough to save Fisk University from closing.

Although it is historical fiction, *A Band of Angels* is based closely on the story of the original Jubilee Singers, whose portraits grace the endpapers of the book. It is not only a book about the past, but about a legacy that continues. The spirituals the original Jubilee Singers sang, and continue to sing today, have become a vibrant part of American culture. And perhaps learning about Ella's determination to get an education will inspire at least one young reader to do the same.

Fannie in the Kitchen Cover

FANNIE IN THE KITCHEN

Fannie in the Kitchen. Illustrated by Nancy Carpenter. Atheneum Books for Young Readers, 2001.

> *"The biggest mistake with griddle cakes," said Fannie, waving her turner,*
> *"is to flip them at the wrong time."*

Fannie Merritt Farmer is sometimes credited with inventing the modern recipe. She was one of the first to publish a book with exact instructions for measuring ingredients in a recipe. But less is known about the real Fannie. She was born in Boston, Massachusetts in 1857. As a young woman, she worked as a mother's helper in the home of Mr. and Mrs. Charles Shaw. Apparently it was there, while teaching young Marcia Shaw to cook, that Fannie came up with the idea of level teaspoons. She went on to become principal of the Boston Cooking School and a well-known author and food expert.

Nancy Carpenter's delightful, humorous artwork combines Victorian etchings with original illustrations.

Illustration from *Fannie in the Kitchen*, page 13. Marcia and Fannie cooking griddle cakes

Girl Wonder Cover

GIRL WONDER: A BASEBALL STORY IN NINE INNINGS

Girl Wonder: A Baseball Story in Nine Innings. Illustrated by Terry Widener. Atheneum Books for Young Readers, 2002.

> *I must have been born to play baseball, because Pop says I was only two when I hurled a corncob at an old tomcat chasing my favorite hen.*

Girl Wonder was inspired by the life of baseball pioneer Alta Weiss, who was born on February 9, 1890, in Ragersville, Ohio. In 1907, at age

Illustration from *Girl Wonder*, page 7

seventeen, Alta began pitching for a semipro all-male team called the Vermilion Independents. She was so successful that the following year her father became a co-owner and the team was renamed the Weiss All-Stars.

Alta Weiss went on to become the only woman in the 1914 graduating class at Starling-Ohio Medical College in Columbus, Ohio. She settled in Norwalk, Ohio and died in 1964.

My daughter, Rebekah, was an avid softball player as she was growing up, and especially enjoyed being a pitcher. This book is dedicated to her.

Apples to Oregon Cover

APPLES TO OREGON

Apples to Oregon: Being the Slightly True Story of How a Brave Pioneer Father Took Apples, Pears, Peaches, Plums and Cherries (and Children) Across the Plains. Illustrated by Nancy Carpenter. Atheneum Books for Young Readers, 2004.

> *My daddy loved growin' apples. And when he got ready to pull up roots and leave Iowa for Oregon, he couldn't bear to leave his apple trees behind.*

Apples to Oregon is a tall tale based on a true-life adventure in the history of fruit! In 1847 Henderson Luelling (which is also sometimes spelled Lewelling) left Salem, Iowa, with his wife, Elizabeth, and eight children. They were headed west on the Oregon Trail, with a wagon carrying seven hundred plants and young trees. Finding enough water for

Windows to the Past: Historical Fiction Picture Books 51

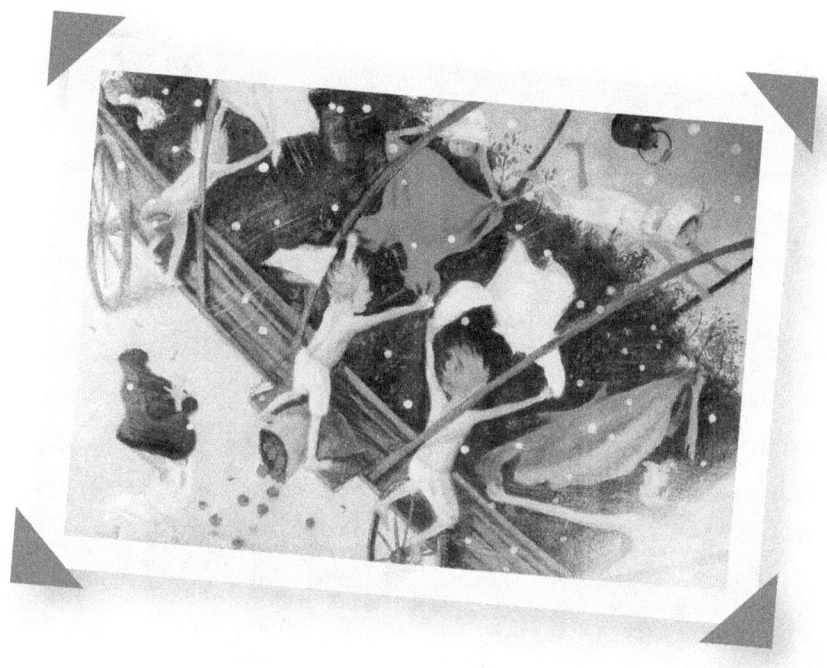

Illustration from *Apples to Oregon*, page 13. Children trying to save plants from hailstorm

this "traveling nursery" must have been a challenge, to say nothing of transporting the heavy "nursery wagons" across rivers. When the family arrived in The Dalles, Oregon, the saplings were loaded onto boats and floated downriver.

The family settled in Milwaukee, Oregon, just south of Portland. Their ninth child, a boy they named Oregon Columbia, was born shortly after they arrived. The Luelling-Meek Nursery, established with Henderson's brother, Seth (who introduced the "Bing" cherry), and William Meek, became the "mother of Oregon nurseries."

Luelling's timing was perfect, and he was able to ship apples at a profit to California to meet the demand after gold was discovered. *Apples to Oregon* won the Western Writers of America's award for storytelling, as well as the Golden Kite award for picture book text. Nancy Carpenter's warm and humorous illustrations never fail to delight readers. One of my favorite experiences was reading in a bookstore where a two-year-old boy trotted up to me and shouted, "Apples, Ho!"

Saving Strawberry Farm Cover

SAVING STRAWBERRY FARM

Saving Strawberry Farm. Illustrated by Rachel Isadora. Greenwillow Books, 2005.

> *The sun was so mean that summer,*
> *it seemed to chase all the clouds away.*

Saving Strawberry Farm takes place during the Great Depression, which affected millions of American families. More than 12 million people lost their jobs when factories, stores, mines, and even banks closed. To make matters worse, the 1930s were years of terrible drought, heat waves, and fierce dust storms.

This book tells the story of a penny auction, which took place when the bank was about to foreclose on a house or farm, and the community stepped in to bid at an auction, keeping the amount so low the original owner could buy back his or her own home. The details of the store that Davey and Rose visit in the story were drawn from two memoirs of the Depression by Robert J. Hastings, who grew up in Marion, Illinois.

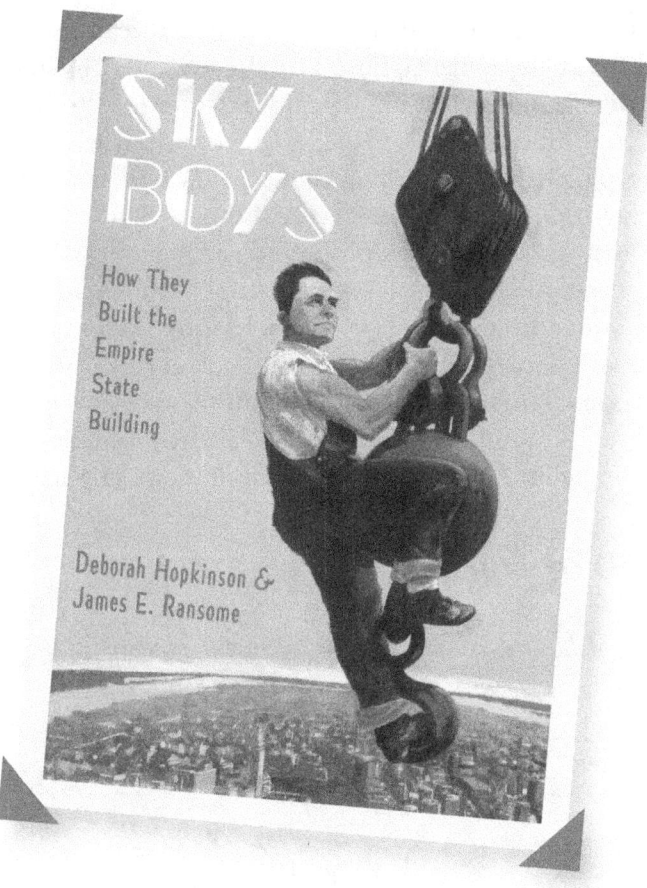

Sky Boys Cover

SKY BOYS

Sky Boys: How They Built the Empire State Building. Illustrated by James E. Ransome. Schwartz & Wade Books, Random House, 2006.

They're getting ready to make something new, bold, soaring.
A symbol of hope in the darkest of times.
A building, clean and simple and straight as a pencil.
And tall.
So tall it will scrape the sky.

Sky Boys was published in 2006, the seventy-fifth anniversary of the opening of one of the nation's most important landmarks: the Empire State Building. One of the most famous buildings in the world, when it was completed in 1931 it immediately became the world's tallest building.

Sky Boys is written in second person: I wanted to capture the feeling of being present at the construction, but also I wanted to find a way to include the details that kids might find fascinating: "sixty thousand tons of steel, ten million bricks ... sixty-five hundred windows, seventy miles of water pipes–"all in one year and forty-five days!"

To this day, the construction of the Empire State Building ranks among the most amazing accomplishments in American architecture. The Empire State Building is 1,250 feet high, with a total height of 1,454 feet if you add the 204-foot-tall television antenna erected in 1950. Millions of people visit the building each year.

James Ransome's rich oil paintings of the workers were inspired by period photographs taken by Lewis Hine. His art truly captures the marvelous strength and agility of the men who made this amazing feat possible.

SWEET LAND OF LIBERTY

Sweet Land of Liberty. Illustrated by Leonard Jenkins. Peachtree Publishers, 2007.

Sweet Land of Liberty Cover

Oscar Chapman grew up in a poor family in Omega, Virginia. His neighbors also struggled to get by. Even the walls of his two-room schoolhouse were bare.

Sweet Land of Liberty recounts the story of Oscar Chapman, who as assistant secretary of the interior helped to make Marian Anderson's historic 1939 Easter concert on the steps of the Lincoln Memorial a reality. In an oral history interview in 1972, Chapman recalled a childhood incident of being expelled from school for bringing a picture of Abraham Lincoln into his classroom. The injustice he witnessed around him, along with his personal experiences, stuck with him, and helped inspire him to work for the cause of equal rights throughout a long and distinguished career in government.

Sweet Land of Liberty explores how events that happen to us as children can have a profound effect on our lives as adults—and sometimes even on the course of history.

MAKING CONNECTIONS

The historical fiction picture books in this section cover many topics and time periods. Here are just a few suggestions of areas for further study:

- Women's History Month (March) activities;
- Notable women scientists and astronomers;
- Lighthouses and the Coast Guard;
- Apples and cooking lessons;
- Women in sports history;
- The history of baseball and/or women and minorities in baseball;
- A study of Reconstruction;
- Historic buildings and landmarks, both locally and nationally;
- The lives of Ella Sheppard Moore and Marian Anderson and the discrimination they faced both as singers and individuals.

FURTHER EXPLORATION

Young readers, parents, and teachers can find a treasure trove of historical fiction picture books, from biographies of little-known explorers and scientists, to accounts of famous (and not-so-famous) historical events. Here are a few of my favorites:

Adler, David A. *The Babe and I*. Illustrated by Terry Widener. Harcourt Brace, 1999.
Atkins, Jeannine. *Mary Anning and the Sea Dragon*. Illustrated by Michael Dooling. Farrar Straus Giroux, 1999.

Bartone, Elisa. *Peppe the Lamplighter.* Illustrated by Ted Lewin. Lothrop, Lee & Shepard, 1993.

Blumberg, Rhoda. *Shipwrecked! The True Adventures of a Japanese Boy.* HarperCollins, 2001.

Brady, Marie. *More Than Anything Else.* Illustrated by Chris K. Soentpiet. Orchard Books, 1995.

Bunting, Eve. *Pop's Bridge.* Illustrated by C.F. Payne. Harcourt, 2006.

McKissack, Pat. *Goin' Someplace Special.* Illustrated by Jerry Pinkney. Atheneum Books for Young Readers, 2001.

Mora, Pat. *Tomás and the Library Lady.* Illustrated by Raul Colon. Knopf: Distributed by Random House, 1997.

Pinkney, Andrea Davis. *Dear Benjamin Banneker.* Illustrated by Brian Pinkney. Harcourt Brace & Co., 1994.

Ryan, Pam Munõz. *When Marian Sang: The True Recital of Marian Anderson: The Voice of a Century.* Illustrated by Brian Selznick. Scholastic Press, 2002.

Wiles, Deborah. *Freedom Summer.* Illustrated by Jerome Lagarrigue. Atheneum Books for Young Readers, 2001.

Chapter Six
Young People in the Tumult of History: Longer Historical Fiction

INTRODUCTION

I enjoy exploring many aspects of history, but I have been especially drawn to nineteenth-century America, a time of dramatic conflict and change. In the North, the industrial revolution transformed cities and drew immigrants from Eastern Europe and Italy to jobs in factories. Regional conflicts over slavery, economics, and westward expansion erupted into the Civil War. All the books in this section take place during these tumultuous times or, in the case of *Hear My Sorrow* and *Into the Firestorm*, in the early years of the twentieth century.

KANSAS BEFORE THE CIVIL WAR: THE PRAIRIE SKIES SERIES

Book One: Pioneer Summer. Illustrated by Patrick Faricy. Aladdin, 2002.

Pioneer Summer Cover

Cabin in the Snow Cover

   Book Two: *Cabin in the Snow*. Illustrated by Patrick Faricy, Aladdin, 2002.
   Book Three: *Our Kansas Home*. Illustrated by Patrick Faricy, Aladdin, 2003.

   Grandpa pulled Charlie close. "I hear they've got big skies our there in Kansas Territory. But it's the same sky that covers us here. If you ask me, the sky's a lot like love. It just spreads out over folks no matter how far apart they are.
   —*Pioneer Summer*

Young People in the Tumult of History: Longer Historical Fiction

Our Kansas Home Cover

I first became interested in the period just before the Civil War while helping my own two children with school history assignments. Memorizing "Kansas-Nebraska Act: 1854" is boring. So I set out to research and write three books that might help young readers imagine what it was like to live during this turbulent period.

I wanted to grapple with questions such as: What were people talking about? What drove the families who left friends and family back East to settle in Kansas? What might it have been like to observe close-up some of the key events that mark this critical time just before the Civil War?

Illustration from *Pioneer Summer*, page 46. Charlie walking next to wagon

Although many aspects of the Prairie Skies Series were inspired by actual events, the main characters are fictional. The story follows Charlie Keller and his family in 1855 as they leave Massachusetts for Lawrence, Kansas. This was a time when people were debating whether slavery should spread to America's territories in the West. The Kansas-Nebraska Act of 1854 created the territories of Kansas and Nebraska. It ended the Missouri Compromise, an agreement in 1820 that forbid slavery in the lands of the Louisiana Purchase except for Missouri, and it changed the law about whether slavery could spread to the territories.

Young People in the Tumult of History: Longer Historical Fiction

Illustration from *Cabin in the Snow*, page 59. Charlie in storm

The Kansas-Nebraska Act established that Kansas would be a free state or a slave state based on how the people in Kansas voted. People from pro-slavery Missouri and free-soil Northerners, like the fictional Keller family, flocked to Kansas to have a voice in the Territory's future. Since the groups wanted different things, they soon clashed. Based on letters and other primary sources, the Prairie Skies Series provides a close-up look at some of the conflicts that led to the Civil War.

THE KLONDIKE GOLD RUSH: THE KLONDIKE KID SERIES

Book One: Sailing for Gold. Illustrated by Bill Farnsworth. Aladdin, 2004.

Book Two: The Long Trail. Illustrated by Bill Farnsworth. Aladdin, 2004.

Book Three: Adventure in Gold Town. Illustrated by Bill Farnsworth. Aladdin, 2004.

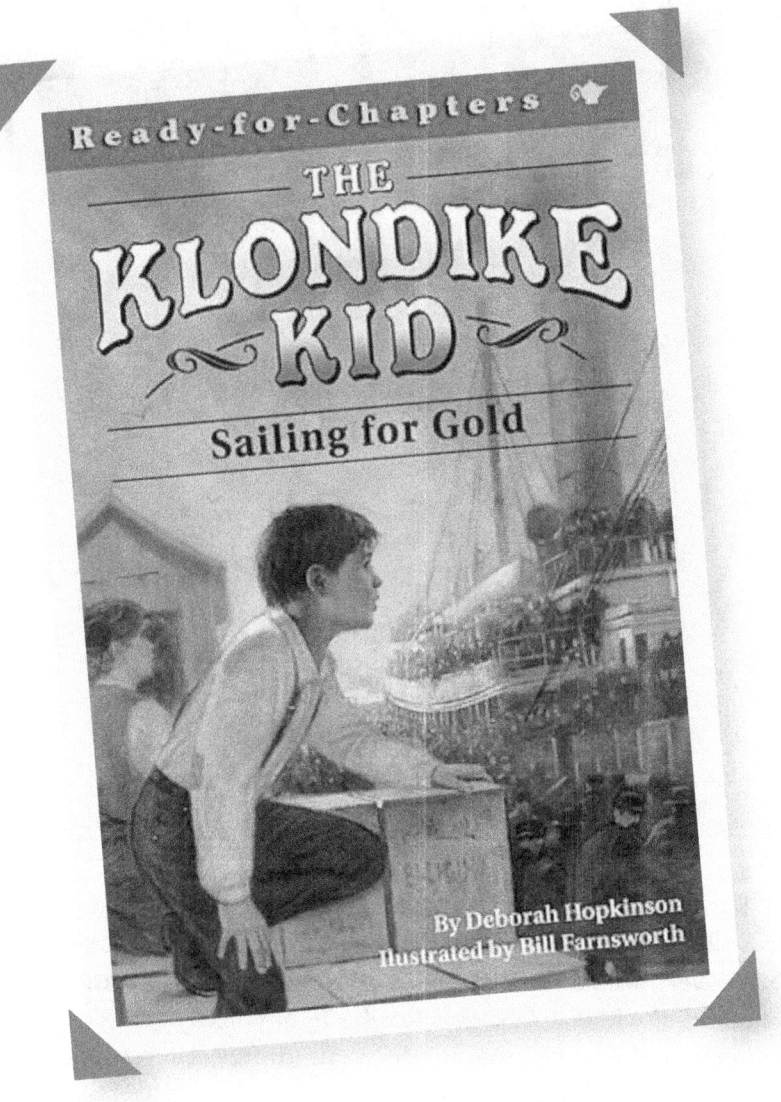

Sailing for Gold Cover

Young People in the Tumult of History: Longer Historical Fiction

The Long Trail Cover

Adventure in Gold Town Cover

Gold! When most folks hear that word, they dream of getting rich. But all I could think of was Uncle Walt. Maybe this was why Uncle Walt hadn't come back.
—*Sailing for Gold*

The Klondike Gold Rush took place at the very end of the nineteenth century. Word of a gold discovery on the Yukon River in Canada's Klondike Valley reached the "Outside" in 1897. When the steamer *Portland* docked in Seattle in July of that year, returning miners had to drag their suitcases down the gangplank because they were so weighted down with gold. The Klondike Gold Rush fired the public imagination, coming at a time when the country was mired in economic depression. Thousands of people caught gold fever, drawn by the promise of riches and adventure.

But just getting to the Klondike was a feat in itself. Men and women journeyed thousands of miles in harsh conditions. The trails to the

Sailing for Gold Image, page 23. Boy holding up newspaper

Klondike are the stuff of legend: the grueling, icy Chilkoot Pass and the horrors of White Pass, sometimes called Dead Horse Trail.

The majority of those who rushed to the Klondike met with disappointment. Some gave up before they reached the boom town of Dawson City. Those that made it that far learned that the richest stakes had been claimed long ago. Others braved the sub-Arctic conditions to try to find gold-bearing gravel on unknown creeks and old stream beds. Still others realized their best chance of making money was to go into business serving the miners themselves.

Dawson City, which grew to 25,000 people almost overnight, became a gold town filled with larger-than-life characters. Just a short while later, in 1899, word came of a gold strike in Nome and the Klondike Gold Rush began to fade.

Adventure in Gold Town Image, page 25. Davey on the river

The Klondike Kid Series follows the adventures of an eleven-year-old boy named Davey Hill, who is living in Seattle when the book begins. Orphaned, he stays in the boardinghouse where he and his widowed mother lived before she died. There he is treated like a servant by Mrs. Tinker, the owner. Davey eventually makes his way to the Klondike. Through his adventures we see not only the world of the prospectors, but also that of the pioneering frontier photographers whose pictures capture the hope—and, in many cases, heartbreak—of the men, women, children, and animals who made the long, harrowing trek into the wilderness.

The Klondike Gold Rush is an immensely exciting period of history and can be studied as part of Westward expansion, in conjunction with the California Gold Rush, and as part of Northwest and Alaska local history units.

THE SHIRTWAIST STRIKE AND THE TRIANGLE FIRE: *DEAR AMERICA, HEAR MY SORROW*

Dear America, Hear My Sorrow: The Diary of Angela Denoto, A Shirtwaist Worker, New York City, 1909. Scholastic, Inc. 2004.

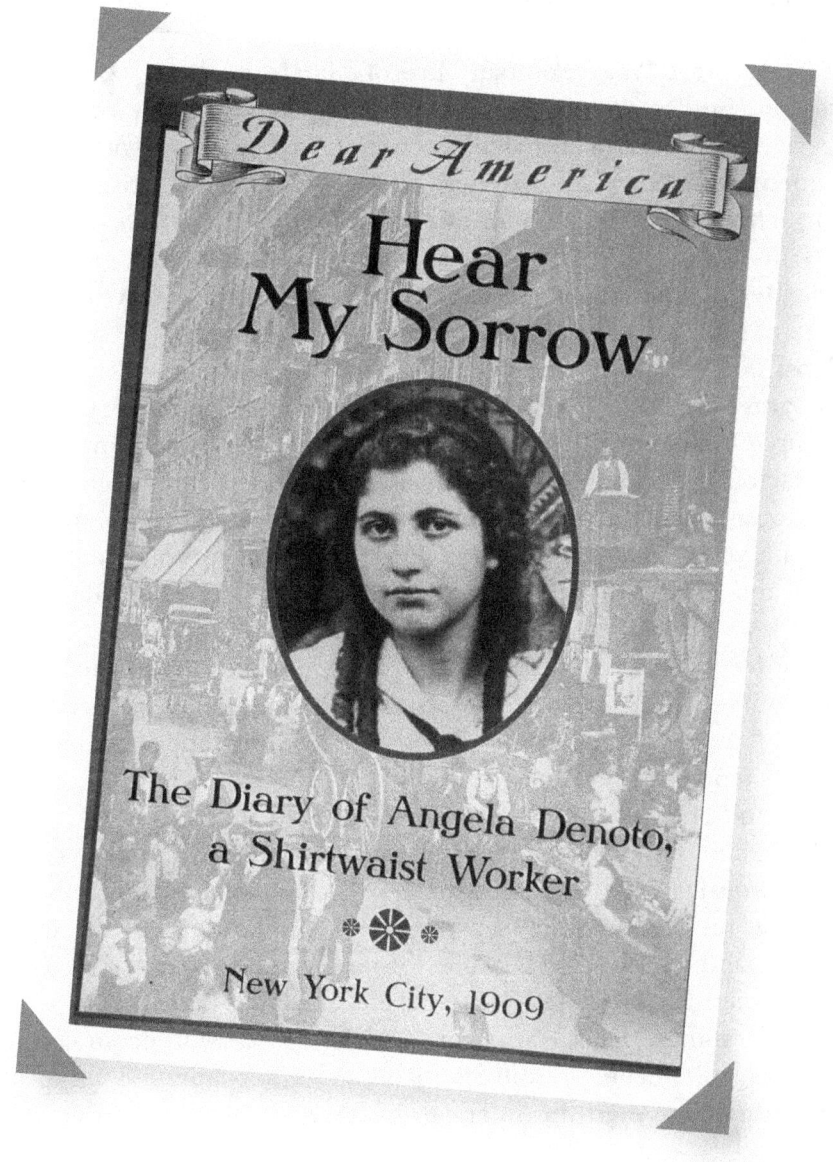

Hear My Sorrow Cover

We held hands and our bodies bumped against one another and we walked in step in the rain. And I thought that if only we could be walking together, maybe we could change something.

Although I've never lived in New York City, I love spending time there. So when I had the opportunity to write about its history for Scholastic's Dear America series, I jumped at the chance. As it turned out, that initial project multiplied into two books: *Hear My Sorrow: The Diary of Angela Denoto, A Shirtwaist Worker, New York City, 1909*, as well as a nonfiction work, *Shutting Out the Sky: Life in the Tenements of New York, 1880–1924*.

The Triangle Waist Company fire of March 25, 1911 stands at the center of *Hear My Sorrow*. But I wanted readers to better understand that event within the context of the emerging garment workers labor movement, including the workers' strike, called the Uprising of the Twenty Thousand, which began in November 1909. Therefore the story begins in the fall of 1909 when a fictitious young Italian girl named Angela Denoto, like many girls at the time, is forced to leave school at the age of fourteen to go to work to help her family.

Most workers in the garment industry were young Jewish and Italian immigrants living on New York City's Lower East Side. By 1910, women made up 70 percent of the approximately 83,000 workers in more than 1,700 factories and small sweatshops. About 600 of these made shirtwaist blouses. Female machine operators generally earned between $7 and $14 a week. Most of the available material I found on the Triangle disaster and the shirtwaist workers strike in 1909 focused on the experience of Jewish immigrants.

In order to better understand the background of my Italian protagonist, I wanted to go beyond the standard history books and academic articles. I read contemporary surveys of immigrant families, and explored tenement housing laws, women's roles, education, family budgets, and children in the work force. I made contact with Dr. Jennifer Guglielmo and Dr. Donna Gabaccia, two contemporary scholars who generously shared their research on Italian immigrants. I also did research at the New York Historical Society, the Museum of the City of New York, and the New York Public Library.

The Triangle fire killed 146 workers, most of them teenage girls and young women. I hope reading *Hear My Sorrow* will encourage people to seek out further resources to better understand this important and heartbreaking event in American history.

THE GREAT SAN FRANCISCO EARTHQUAKE AND FIRE: *INTO THE FIRESTORM: A NOVEL OF SAN FRANCISCO, 1906*

Into the Firestorm: A Novel of San Francisco, 1906. Alfred A. Knopf, 2006.

Into the Firestorm Cover

For a second, the shaking let up. Then it started in again, violent and more twisting. An image flashed through Nick's mind of Gran wringing clothes over the wash tin with her tough, strong hands. That was it. The earth was being wrung out of shape.

The San Francisco earthquake occurred at 5:13 A.M. on Wednesday, April 18, 1906. Although contemporary accounts put the death toll much lower, it is now estimated that about 3,000 people died, primarily as a result of collapsing buildings. Most of the physical damage to the city occurred not from the quake itself, but in three days of raging fires.

One newspaper account of stories of the disaster was of a boy named Nicholas Dray, who had apparently escaped from a county poor farm and had been taken in by a local merchant just a few days before the fire. Left alone while his new employer was away on business, Nick braved a soldier's gun to rescue the man's dog, Brownie. Supposedly the boy said, "He is a very good dog." In my novel, I add other characters, including a boy named Tommy, based on Hugh Kwong Lian, who lived in Chinatown at the time of the disaster.

I decided to set the story in an area of San Francisco near the Appraiser's Building, one of the few downtown buildings not demolished in the fire. That building was near the Hoteling Whiskey Company, and first-hand accounts contain a vivid description of the successful effort to save the warehouse. To research *Into the Firestorm*, I relied on excellent primary sources, including letters, photographs, and eyewitness accounts. I also traveled to San Francisco to walk around Jackson Square, the story's setting.

MAKING CONNECTIONS

Here are some ideas for other topics to look at with the books in this section:

- Conflicts between Native Americans and white settlers;
- Daily life on the prairie;
- The abolition movement;
- Regional differences and conflicts between the North and the South;
- Difference between Klondike Gold Rush and California Gold Rush;
- Differences in life in northern industrial cities and the rural South;
- Factory workers and the rise of the labor movement;
- Life in big cities now and then: what do we do today to prepare for disasters like earthquakes and fires?

FURTHER EXPLORATION

This section includes both historical fiction and nonfiction books which may be of interest.

Kansas and Prairie Settler Life

McMullan, Kate. *My America. As Far as I Can See: Meg's Diary, St. Louis to the Kansas Territory, 1856.* Scholastic, 2001.

Williams, David. *Grandma Essie's Covered Wagon.* Illustrated by Wiktor Sadowski. Knopf: Distributed by Random House, 1993.

The Klondike Gold Rush

Hobbs, Will. *Jason's Gold.* Morrow Junior Books, 1999.

Hobbs, Will. *Down the Yukon.* HarperCollins, 2001.

Murphy, Claire Rudolph and Jane G. Haigh. *Children of the Gold Rush.* Roberts Rinehart Publishers, 1999.

Murphy, Claire Rudolph and Jane G. Haigh. *Gold Rush Dogs.* Alaska Northwest Books, 2001.

San Francisco Earthquake and Fire

Karwoski, Gail. *Quake!: Disaster in San Francisco, 1906.* Illustrated by Robert Papp. Peachtree Publishers, 2004.

Hansen, Gladys C. and Emmet Condon. *Denial of Disaster.* Cameron and Co., 1989.

Yep, Lawrence. *Dragonwings.* Harper & Row, 1977.

Yep, Lawrence. *The Earth Dragon Awakes: The San Francisco Earthquake of 1906.* HarperCollins Publishers, 2006.

Triangle Strike and Fire

Auch, Mary Jane. *Ashes of Roses.* H. Holt, 2002.

Dash, Joan. *We Shall Not Be Moved: The Women's Factory Strike of 1909.* Scholastic, 1996.

McClymer, John F. *The Triangle Strike and Fire.* Harcourt Brace College Publishers, 1998.

Chapter Seven
Real People, Real Lives

INTRODUCTION

I love looking at old black-and-white photographs, especially ones of children, or men and women at work. They always make me want to learn more about the people staring back at me and what their lives were like.

This fascination led me to write two longer nonfiction works. *Shutting Out the Sky* focuses on the lives of immigrants on the Lower East Side of New York, while *Up Before Daybreak* explores the history of the many children, men, and women involved in the cotton industry in America. Both books include a large selection of photographs and have short sections that can be read aloud and hopefully enjoyed by readers young and old.

LIFE ON THE LOWER EAST SIDE: *SHUTTING OUT THE SKY*

Shutting Out the Sky: Life in the Tenements of New York, 1880–1924. Scholastic, 2004.

> *Maurice Hindus was fourteen when he came to New York from a small village in Russia. He'd never lived in a big city before, and he looked around in wonder at everything he saw....*
>
> *As he walked through the teeming streets, Maurice was bursting with questions: Where did all these people come from? What did they talk about at home? What did they eat? Maurice was eager to talk to all these strangers, but he couldn't. He didn't speak any English.*

Between 1880 and 1919, about 23 million people, most from Eastern and Southern Europe, came to the United States. Many settled in New York City's Lower East Side, a burgeoning center for the ready-to-wear garment industry. Yet with such great numbers of people, it's sometimes hard to grasp the fact that each person was an individual, with his or her own family, culture, language, and story.

Shutting Out the Sky tells the story of immigrant life through the voices of five young people. The focus is both on the overall history as well as aspects of daily life, and the book includes chapters on coming to America, the immigrants' first impressions, education, work, and family life.

My research included several trips to New York City to search through photo archives at the New York Historical Society, the Museum

Shutting Out the Sky Cover

of the City of New York, and the New York Public Library. I walked the neighborhoods, listened to oral history tapes of immigrants at New York University, and read every book I could get my hands on. The period photographs in *Shutting Out the Sky* help to bring to life the details of daily life, showing kids making a fort on a fire escape, working as messenger boys, or playing in the streets.

Shutting Out the Sky is organized chronologically, showing how families desired to come to America, the journey across the Atlantic, and the issues that children and adults of the time would deal with: work, going to school, learning a new language, and the process of becoming an American while maintaining their first culture.

Many of us can trace our family histories back to Ellis Island, others belong to families that have come to this country more recently. Immigration, voluntary or forced, is a major theme of United States history, and a topic that we will return to again and again. I hope this book is a useful addition to what is already a rich array of resources—nonfiction, fiction, and primary sources—as we all seek to make sense of our past, our present, and our future.

Shutting Out the Sky includes a timeline, a detailed bibliography, and a special section on further reading geared toward young readers. The book's awards include a Jane Addams Peace Award Honor Award, NCTE Orbis Pictus Honor Award, IRA Teachers' Choice selection, and James Madison Award Honor.

COTTON IN AMERICA: *UP BEFORE DAYBREAK*

Up Before Daybreak: Cotton and People in America. Scholastic Nonfiction, 2006.

Up Before Daybreak Cover

Boott Cotton Mills Museum in Lowell, Massachusetts. (Deborah Hopkinson)

The story of cotton is the history of countless ordinary individuals, whose names, songs, hopes, and fears are, for the most part, lost to time.

Although I grew up in the cotton mill town of Lowell, Massachusetts, I didn't fully appreciate the role of cotton in American history until I began working on this book. In fact, it would be hard to underestimate the impact of cotton on America. Cotton is linked to the industrial revolution in the North, and the reliance on slavery in the South. Despite advances in technology in other areas, cotton was the last major crop to make the transition from hand labor to machine labor.

What fascinated me most was how the cotton industry affected the lives of individuals. For cotton touched the lives of countless generations of slaves and sharecroppers, migrant field laborers, mill workers, and sewing machine operators.

Up Before Daybreak is divided into two parts: before the Civil War and after. While it's clearly impossible to cover the entire history of cotton in one book, I hope that through stories, facts, photographs, and oral history, readers will come away with a solid introduction to the role of cotton in American history. Individual chapters focus on how cotton came to America, its role in the growth of slavery and the economy, the growth of the Lowell mills, and the advent of the sharecropping system and Southern mills after the Civil War.

I also hope *Up Before Daybreak* will help young people appreciate our history more fully by seeing pictures and hearing the voices of children in the past. *Up Before Daybreak* received starred reviews in *Kirkus*, *School Library Journal*, and *Booklist*, and was named an ALA Notable book. It also was named a Carter G. Woodson Award Honor Book by the National Council for the Social Studies.

MAKING CONNECTIONS

Both *Shutting Out the Sky* and *Up Before Daybreak* can be used to explore many other subject areas, including:

- New York City history;
- Ellis Island and family history;
- Immigration in America now and then;
- Child labor and education;
- Factories and farm workers;
- The differences between life in cities and farms;
- Workplace safety and the rights of workers;
- Labor unions;
- Slavery.

FURTHER EXPLORATION

Shutting Out the Sky

Auch, Mary Jane. *Ashes of Roses*. H. Holt, 2002.
Bartoletti, Susan Campbell. *Kids on Strike!* Houghton Mifflin, 1999.
Bial, Raymond. *Tenement: Immigrant Life on the Lower East Side*. Houghton Mifflin, 2002.
Dash, Joan. *We Shall Not Be Moved: The Women's Factory Strike of 1909*. Scholastic, 1996.
Freedman, Russell. *Kids at Work: Lewis Hine and the Crusade against Child Labor*. Clarion Books, 1994.
Freeman, Russell. *Immigrant Kids*. Dutton, 1980.
Lasky, Katherine. *Dreams in the Golden Country: The Diary of Zipporah Feldman, a Jewish Immigrant Girl*. Scholastic, 1998.
Kisseloff, Jeff. *You Must Remember This: An Oral History of Manhattan from the 1890s to World War II*. Harcourt Brace Jovanovich, 1989.

McClymer, John F. *The Triangle Strike and Fire*. Harcourt Brace College Publishers, 1998.

Riis, Jacob. *How the Other Half Lives. Studies among the Tenements of New York*. Charles Scribner's Sons, 1890.

Up Before Daybreak

Boling, Katharine. *January 1905*. Harcourt, 2004.

Paterson, Katherine. *Lyddie*. Lodestar Books, 1991.

McCully, Emily Arnold. *The Bobbin Girl*. Dial Books for Young Readers, 1996.

McKissack, Pat C. and McKissack, Fredrick. *Christmas in the Big House, Christmas in the Quarters*. Illustrated by John Thompson. Scholastic, 1994.

Williams, Sherley Anne. *Working Cotton*. Illustrated by Carole M. Byard. Harcourt Brace Jovanovich, 1992.

Chapter Eight
Bluebirds in the Garden: Two Picture Books Celebrating the Natural World

INTRODUCTION

Sometimes stories take shape in surprising ways. These two picture books, both illustrated by Idaho artist Bethanne Anderson, were written while I lived in Walla Walla, a picturesque town nestled against the foothills of the Blue Mountains in the wheat and wine growing region of eastern Washington State. Both grew out of my own experiences: seeing a bluebird for the first time and my love of gardening.

BLUEBIRD SUMMER

Bluebird Summer. Illustrated by Bethanne Anderson. Greenwillow, 2001.

Bluebird Summer Cover

Every summer my little brother, Cody, and I go to the farm on the ridge. It's not much of a farm anymore. The wheat fields are still there, washing up against the barn like a golden sea, but they belong to someone else now. Since Grandma died, Gramps has sold them off, one by one.

This book was inspired by seeing my first bluebird in the rolling hills of eastern Washington, where we lived for ten years. A Golden Kite Award Honor Book for Picture Book Text, it tells the story of Mags and Cody, a brother and sister who usually spend the summer on their grandparents' farm. Bethanne Anderson's luminous illustrations depict Gramps and the children as they attempt to cope with Grandma's death, and find ways to keep her spirit alive through the garden and bluebirds she loved.

When sharing this book with students in schools, I sometimes bring a bluebird nesting box with me, and share photographs of how communities come together to make and maintain bluebird trails to protect and support these beautiful songbirds. My Web site also includes links to the North American Bluebird Society for people seeking more information about bluebird conservation.

Bluebird Summer was named a Notable Children's Books in the Language Arts and a Notable Social Studies Trade Book for Young People, as well as one of the Best Children's Books of the Year by Bank Street College of Education.

A PACKET OF SEEDS

A Packet of Seeds. Illustrated by Bethanne Anderson. Greenwillow, 2004.

All Pa could see was the new land before him. All Momma could feel was the sorrow of leaving everything behind.

Our house in Walla Walla was on a half acre of land, and soon after we arrived, I began to garden seriously for the first time in my life. Trying to transform our little patch of land gave me a new appreciation of gardens and the comfort and joy flowers can bring. If you drive along the back roads of rural eastern Washington, you often come across old, isolated farmhouses, surrounded by acres of open fields. But the houses almost always have beautiful front gardens, and flowers lining the driveway. Seeing these houses, I couldn't help imagining what life was like for those families who took part in westward expansion, leaving behind friends, communities, and, of course, their beloved gardens.

A Packet of Seeds Cover

A Packet of Seeds follows one such family. Mary and James and their two children, Jim and Annie, set out to homestead on the prairie. Annie is worried about how sad and lonely her pregnant mother seems. When spring comes, and her baby sister arrives, Annie sets out to find a way to help her mother feel more at home in their new life.

A Packet of Seeds includes an author's notes about the roses women carried with them on the Oregon Trail, including Harrison's Yellow. The book received a starred review in *Kirkus* and was listed in the Cooperative Children's Book Center's Choices for 2005.

MAKING CONNECTIONS

Here are some suggestions for using these books to explore other subjects and areas of learning:

- Habitat loss and biodiversity;
- The effort to save the Eastern Bluebirds;
- Building bluebird boxes;

- Community gardens;
- Learning about indigenous plants;
- Heirloom roses.

FURTHER EXPLORATION

Bluebird Summer

Chrustowski, Rick. *Blue Sky Bluebird.* Henry Holt and Co., 2004.
Heilman, Joan Rattner. *Bluebird Rescue.* Lothrop, Lee & Shepard Books, 1982.
Stokes, Donald W. and Lillian Q. *The Bluebird Book: The Complete Guide to Attracting Bluebirds.* Little, Brown, 1991.

A Packet of Seeds

Bunting, Eve. *Dandelions.* Illustrated by Greg Shed. Harcourt Brace, 1995.
Calkins, Erica. *Hatchet, Hands & Hoe: Planting the Pioneer Spirit: A Bushel of Practical Nostalgia.* Caxton Printers, 1996.
Warren, Andrea. *Pioneer Girl: Growing Up on the Prairie.* Morrow Junior Books, 1998.
Schlissel, Lillian. *Women's Diaries of the Westward Journey.* Schocken Books, 1992.

Chapter Nine
Biographies of Memorable People

INTRODUCTION

These nonfiction biographies introduce three extraordinary historical figures to young readers. In writing about these well-known people, I wanted to focus on some of the childhood events that shaped their adult lives. For instance, as a girl Susan B. Anthony challenged the notion that one of the women workers in her father's small mill could not be made a boss. From an early age, Charles Darwin developed a love of nature and habits of close observation of the natural world. John Adams grew up with a strong sense of home and place.

I hope these introductory works will spark an interest in readers, and, in addition to including titles for children in the Further Exploration section, I've also listed some outstanding adult resources.

JOHN ADAMS

John Adams Speaks for Freedom. Illustrated by Craig Orback. Aladdin, 2005.

> *"The Revolution was in the minds and hearts of the people."*
> —John Adams

This Ready-to-Read biography for Level 3 young readers traces the life of our nation's second president, John Adams. Born in 1735 in Braintree, Massachusetts, Adams and his "Dearest Friend" Abigail had four children by 1774, when he was chosen as a delegate to the first Continental Congress. This thirty-two-page biography highlights dramatic episodes such as the dangerous ocean journey to France that

John Adams Cover

Illustration from *John Adams Speaks for Freedom*, page 16. Adams in Philadelphia

Adams made with his ten-year-old son, John Quincy, in 1778. John Adams and the nation's third president, Thomas Jefferson, both died on July 4, 1826.

SUSAN B. ANTHONY

Susan B. Anthony: Fighter for Women's Rights. Illustrated by Amy Bates. Aladdin, 2005.

"Failure is impossible."

—Susan B. Anthony

Susan B. Anthony: Fighter for Women's Rights Cover

Susan B. Anthony was born on February 15, 1820, in Adams, Massachusetts. This Ready-to-Read Level 3 biography introduces young readers to her extraordinary life and her struggle to obtain the right to vote for American women. Beginning with her childhood, it chronicles her fateful meeting in 1851 with Elizabeth Cady Stanton and their lifelong partnership and friendship. Illustrated in full color, this book includes five short chapters and a brief timeline of the major events and accomplishments until her death in 1906.

Illustration from *Susan B. Anthony: Fighter for Women's Rights*, page 4. Failure is impossible

CHARLES DARWIN

Who Was Charles Darwin? Illustrated by Nancy Harrison. Grosset & Dunlap, 2005.

> "... from so simple a beginning endless forms most beautiful and most wonderful have been, and are being evolved."
>
> —Charles Darwin

Charles Darwin was born on February 12, 1809, on the same day as Abraham Lincoln. This reader-friendly 104-page biography includes

Who Was Charles Darwin? Cover

numerous black-and-white illustrations that bring to life some of the major incidents in Darwin's life. Nine chapters encompass Darwin's boyhood love of collecting and nature, his schooling, and, of course, his famous five-year voyage on the *H.M.S. Beagle*. Darwin was a dedicated father and husband, and the book includes several anecdotes about family life at Down House. Darwin's discovery of the theory of evolution by natural selection is also covered, along with short breakout sections that profile some of Darwin's famous contemporaries, including Alfred Russel Wallace.

The book includes both a timeline of Darwin's life and a corresponding timeline of world events. There is also a short bibliography and a listing of Web sites for further information.

MAKING CONNECTIONS

Here are some ideas for making connections between the books in this section and other topics:

- The Continental Congress;
- The life of Abigail Adams;
- Why America fought for independence;
- History of the struggle for women's rights;
- History of science and the study of evolution;
- Evolution and biology today.

FURTHER EXPLORATION

John and Abigail Adams

Adkins, Jan. *John Adams, Young Revolutionary.* Illustrated by Meryl Henderson. Aladdin, 2002.
Bober, Natalie. *Abigail Adams: Witness to a Revolution.* Atheneum Books for Young Readers, 1995.
Harness, Cheryl. *The Revolutionary John Adams.* National Geographic, 2003.
McCullough, David G. *John Adams.* Simon & Schuster, 2001.
Wagoner, Jean Brown. *Abigail Adams: Girl of Colonial Days.* Illustrated by James. J. Ponter. Aladdin, 1992.

Susan B. Anthony

Bausum, Ann. *With Courage and Cloth: Winning the Fight for a Woman's Right to Vote.* National Geographic, 2004.
Fritz, Jean. *You Want Women to Vote, Lizzie Stanton?* Illustrated by DyAnne DiSalvo.
McCully, Emily Arnold. *The Ballot Box Battle.* Knopf, 1996.
Monsell, Helen Albee. *Susan B. Anthony: Champion of Women's Rights.* Aladdin, 1986.

Charles Darwin

Browne, E.J. *Charles Darwin: A Biography. Volume I: Voyaging. Volume 2: The Power of Place.* Knopf: Distributed by Random House, 1995–2002.
Macdonald, Fiona. *Inside the Beagle with Charles Darwin.* Illustrated by Mark Bergin. Enchanted Lion Books, 2005.
Sis, Peter. *The Tree of Life: A Book Depicting the Life of Charles Darwin, Naturalist, Geologist & Thinker.* Farrar Straus Giroux, 2003.
Stefoff, Rebecca. *Charles Darwin and the Evolution Revolution.* Oxford University Press, 1998.

Appendices

Appendices

Bibliography

CHRONOLOGICAL LISTING OF DEBORAH HOPKINSON'S BOOKS AND AWARDS

Sweet Clara and the Freedom Quilt. Illustrated by James Ransome. Alfred A. Knopf, 1993.

> International Reading Association Award
> Reading Rainbow Book
> Children's Book-of-the-Month Club
> A notable trade book in the field of social studies
> Jefferson Cup Award Honor Book

Birdie's Lighthouse. Illustrated by Kimberly Bulcken Root. Atheneum Books for Young Readers, 1997.

> Parents Choice Silver Honor Book
> BCCB Blue Ribbon Book
> A Junior Library Guild Selection
> Best Children's Books of the Year, 1998; Bank Street College of Education.

Maria's Comet. Illustrated by Deborah Lanino. Atheneum Books for Young Readers, 1999.

A Band of Angels. Illustrated by Raul Colon. Atheneum Books for Young Readers, 1999.

> SCBWI Golden Kite Award for Picture Book Text
> Jane Addams Award Honor Book
> ALA Notable Book
> *Smithsonian Magazine* Notable Book
> *Publishers Weekly* Best Book of 1999
> A Junior Library Guild Selection
> NCTE Books for a Global Society
> Featured on NPR's "Saturday Morning Edition"
> Starred Reviews: *Kirkus, Booklist, Publishers Weekly, School Library Journal*

Bluebird Summer. Illustrated by Bethanne Anderson. Greenwillow Books, 2001.

> A Junior Library Guild Selection
> A notable trade book in the field of social studies
> Golden Kite Award Honor Book for Picture Book Text
> Honor Book, Ohio Farm Bureau Federation Children's Book Award
> NCTE Notable Book in the Language Arts

Fannie in the Kitchen. Illustrated by Nancy Carpenter. Atheneum Books for Young Readers, 2001.

    A Junior Library Guild Selection
    A *Publishers Weekly* Best Book of 2001
    Smithsonian Magazine Notable Book
    Parenting Magazine Reading Magic Book
    Children's Crown Award Honor Book
    Starred Reviews: *Kirkus, Booklist, Publishers Weekly, School Library Journal*

Under the Quilt of Night. Illustrated by James E. Ransome. Atheneum Books for Young Readers, 2001.

    The Paterson Prize for Books for Young People
    IRA/CBC Children's Choices 2003
    Washington State Book Award 2003 Winner
    Starred Reviews: *Kirkus, Publishers Weekly, School Library Journal*

The Prairie Skies Series.

    Book One: Pioneer Summer. Illustrated by Patrick Faricy. Aladdin, 2002.
    Book Two: Cabin in the Snow. Illustrated by Patrick Faricy, Aladdin, 2002.
    Book Three: Our Kansas Home. Illustrated by Patrick Faricy, Aladdin, 2003.

Girl Wonder: A Baseball Story in Nine Innings. Illustrated by Terry Widener. Atheneum Books for Young Readers, 2003.

    Parents Choice Gold Award
    Junior Library Guild selection
    Great Lakes Book Award
    Oppenheim Toy Portfolio Gold Award
    Jane Addams Peace Award Honor Book
    Notable Social Studies Trade Books for Young People, 2004.
    Choices, 2004; Cooperative Children's Book Center.

Shutting Out the Sky: Life in the Tenements of New York 1880–1924. Orchard Books, 2003.

    James Madison Book Award Honor
    Book Links "Lasting Connections"
    Booklist Editors' Choice
    CCBC Choices selection
    IRA Teacher's Choice
    Jane Addams Peace Award Honor
    NCSS/CBC Notable Social Studies Trade Book for Young People
    NCTE Orbis Pictus Honor
    New York Public Library 100 Titles for Reading and Sharing
    New York Public Library Book for the Teen Age
    Sydney Taylor Notable Book

A Packet of Seeds. Illustrated by Bethanne Andersen. Greenwillow Books, 2004.
Choices. Cooperative Children's Book Center, 2005.

Apples to Oregon: Being the (Slightly) True Narrative of How a Brave Pioneer Father Brought Apples, Peaches, Pears, Plums, Grapes, and Cherries (and Children) Across the Plains. Illustrated by Nancy Carpenter. Atheneum Books for Young Readers, 2004.

Publishers Weekly Best Children's Books, 2004.
A Junior Library Guild Selection
SCBWI Golden Kite Award for Picture Book Text
ALA Notable Book
Oppenheim Toy Portfolio Platinum Award
Western Writers of America Spur Award for Storytelling
Oregon Book Award Finalist
Starred Reviews: *Kirkus, Publishers Weekly,* and *School Library Journa*
Best Children's Books of the Year. Bank Street College of Education, 2004.

Dear America, Hear My Sorrow: The Diary of Angela Denoto, A Shirtwaist Worker, New York City, 1909. Scholastic, Inc. 2004.

The Klondike Kid.

Book One: Sailing for Gold. Illustrated by Bill Farnsworth. Aladdin, 2004.
Texas Bluebonnet Award Nominee. 2005–06.
Book Two: The Long Trail. Illustrated by Bill Farnsworth. Aladdin, 2004.
Book Three: Adventure in Gold Town. Illustrated by Bill Farnsworth. Aladdin, 2004.

Who Was Charles Darwin? Illustrated by Nancy Harrison.Grosset & Dunlap, 2005.

Billy and the Rebel: Based on a True Civil War Story. Illustrated by Brian Floca. Atheneum Books for Young Readers, 2005.
Best Children's Books of the Year. Bank Street College of Education, 2005.

From Slave to Solider: Based on a True Civil War Story. Illustrated by Brian Floca. Atheneum Books for Young Readers, 2005.

Oppenheim Toy Portfolio Gold Award
Best Children's Books of the Year. Bank Street College of Education, 2007.
Choices. Cooperative Children's Book Center, 2006.

Stories of Famous Americans: John Adams Speaks for Freedom. Illustrated by Craig Orback. Aladdin, 2005.
Best Children's Books of the Year. Bank Street College of Education, 2005.
Choices. Cooperative Children's Book Center, 2006.

Saving Strawberry Farm. Illustrated by Rachel Isadora. Greenwillow Books, 2005.

Stories of Famous Americans: Susan B. Anthony: Fighter for Women's Rights. Illustrated by Amy Bates. Aladdin, 2005.

Sky Boys: How They Built the Empire State Building. Illustrated by James E. Ransome. Schwartz & Wade Books, 2006.

>*Choices.* Cooperative Children's Book Center, 2007.
>Boston Globe-Horn Book Honor Award
>ALA Notable Book
>Oregon Book Award Finalist
>*Best Children's Books of the Year.* Bank Street College of Education, 2007.

Up Before Daybreak: Cotton and People in America. Scholastic Nonfiction, 2006.

>*Choices.* Cooperative Children's Book Center, 2007.
>A Junior Library Guild Selection.
>ALA Notable Book
>*School Library Journal,* Best Books 2006.
>Best Books for Young Adults, 2007
>*Best Children's Books of the Year.* Bank Street College of Education, 2007.
>School Library Journal Book Review Stars, 2006
>Carter G. Woodson Honor Award, National Council for the Social Studies

Into the Firestorm: A Novel of San Francisco, 1906. Alfred A. Knopf, 2006.

The Best Children's Books of the Year. Bank Street College of Education, 2007.
New York Library Books for the Teenage

Sweet Land of Liberty. Illustrated by Leonard Jenkins. Peachtree Press, 2007.

Photo Credits

Photo of Deborah Hopkinson during a school visit by Dimitri Thomas from the Thomas/Hopkinson Family Album. Reprinted courtesy of Dimitri Thomas and Deborah Hopkinson.

Photo of Gloria and Russell Hopkinson from the Hopkinson Family Album. Courtesy of Deborah Hopkinson.

Photo of Gloria and Russell Hopkinson and Deborah Hopkinson from the Hopkinson Family Album. Courtesy of Deborah Hopkinson.

Photo of Deborah Hopkinson at one year from the Hopkinson Family Album. Courtesy of Deborah Hopkinson.

Photo of Deborah Hopkinson at age two from the Hopkinson Family Album. Courtesy of Deborah Hopkinson.

Photo of Rebekah Hopkinson by Deborah Hopkinson from the Hopkinson Family Album. Courtesy of Deborah Hopkinson.

Photo of Deborah Hopkinson with doll carriage from the Hopkinson Family Album. Courtesy of Deborah Hopkinson.

Photo of elementary school by Deborah Hopkinson from the Hopkinson Family Album. Courtesy of Deborah Hopkinson.

Photo of Deborah Hopkinson at Lowell High School by Dimitri Thomas from the Thomas/Hopkinson Family Album. Reprinted courtesy of Dimitri Thomas and Deborah Hopkinson.

Photo of Andrew Thomas and Deborah Hopkinson by Dimitri Thomas from the Thomas/Hopkinson Family Album. Reprinted courtesy of Dimitri Thomas, Andrew Thomas, and Deborah Hopkinson.

Photo of Dimitri Thomas and Kona by Deborah Hopkinson from the Thomas/Hopkinson Family Album. Reprinted courtesy of Dimitri Thomas and Deborah Hopkinson.

Photo of Rebekah Hopkinson and Andy Thomas by Deborah Hopkinson from the Thomas/Hopkinson Family Album. Reprinted with permission.

Photo of Deborah Hopkinson by Dimitri Thomas from the Thomas/Hopkinson Family Album. Reprinted courtesy of Dimitri Thomas and Deborah Hopkinson.

Photo of Dimitri Thomas from the Thomas/Hopkinson Family Album. Reprinted courtesy of Dimitri Thomas and Deborah Hopkinson.

Photo of Jubilee Singers exhibit by Deborah Hopkinson from the Thomas/Hopkinson Family Album. Reprinted courtesy of Deborah Hopkinson.

Photo of Alta Weiss exhibit by Deborah Hopkinson from the Thomas/Hopkinson Family Album. Reprinted courtesy of Deborah Hopkinson.

Photo of Jubilee Hall by Deborah Hopkinson from the Thomas/Hopkinson Family Album. Reprinted courtesy of Deborah Hopkinson.

Photo of Jubilee Hall historical marker by Deborah Hopkinson from the Thomas/Hopkinson Family Album. Reprinted courtesy of Deborah Hopkinson.

Photo of Deborah Hopkinson by Michele Hill from the Thomas/Hopkinson Family Album. Reprinted with permission.

Sweet Clara and the Freedom Quilt. Jacket art © 1993 by James Ransome, written by Deborah Hopkinson. Used by permission of Alfred A. Knopf, Inc., an imprint of Random House, Inc.

Cover art and interior art from *Under the Quilt of Night* by Deborah Hopkinson, Illustrated by James E. Ransome. Reprinted with the permission of Atheneum Books for Young Readers, an imprint of Simon & Schuster Children's Publishing Division from *Under the Quilt of Night* by Deborah Hopkinson, illustrated by James E. Ransome. Text Copyright © 2002 Deborah Hopkinson. Illustrations copyright © 2002 James E. Ransome.

Cover art and interior art from *Billy and the Rebel: Based on a True Civil War Story* by Deborah Hopkinson, Illustrated by Brian Floca. Reprinted with the permission of Atheneum Books for Young Readers, an imprint of Simon & Schuster Children's Publishing Division from *Billy and the Rebel, Based on a True Civil War Story* by Deborah Hopkinson, illustrated by Brian Floca. Text Copyright © 2005 Deborah Hopkinson. Illustrations copyright © 2005 Brian Floca.

Cover art and interior art from *From Slave to Soldier: Based on a True Civil War Story* by Deborah Hopkinson, Illustrated by Brian Floca. Reprinted with the permission of Atheneum Books for Young Readers, an imprint of Simon & Schuster Children's Publishing Division from *From Slave to Soldier: Based on a True Civil War Story* by Deborah Hopkinson, illustrated by Brian Floca. Text Copyright © 2005 Deborah Hopkinson. Illustrations copyright © 2005 Brian Floca.

Cover art and interior art from *Birdie's Lighthouse* by Deborah Hopkinson, Illustrated by Kimberly Bulcken Root. Reprinted with the permission of Atheneum Books for Young Readers, an imprint of Simon & Schuster Children's Publishing Division from *Birdie's Lighthouse* by Deborah Hopkinson, illustrated by Kimberly Bulcken Root. Text Copyright © 1997 Deborah Hopkinson. Illustrations copyright © 1997 Kimberly Bulcken Root.

Cover art and interior art from *Maria's Comet* by Deborah Hopkinson, Illustrated by Deborah Lanino. Reprinted with the permission of Atheneum Books for Young Readers, an imprint of Simon & Schuster Children's Publishing Division from *Maria's Comet* by Deborah Hopkinson, illustrated by Kimberly Bulcken Root. Text Copyright © 1999 Deborah Hopkinson. Illustrations copyright © 1999 Deborah Lanino.

Cover art and interior art from *A Band of Angels* by Deborah Hopkinson, Illustrated by Raul Colon. Reprinted with the permission of Atheneum Books for Young Readers, an imprint of Simon & Schuster Children's Publishing Division from *A Band of Angels* by Deborah Hopkinson, illustrated by Raul Colon. Text Copyright © 1999 Deborah Hopkinson. Illustrations copyright © 1999 Raul Colon.

Cover art and interior art from *Fannie in the Kitchen* by Deborah Hopkinson, Illustrated by Nancy Carpenter. Reprinted with the permission of Atheneum Books for Young Readers, an imprint of Simon & Schuster Children's Publishing Division from *Fannie in the Kitchen* by Deborah Hopkinson, illustrated by Nancy Carpenter. Text Copyright © 2001 Deborah Hopkinson. Illustrations copyright © 2001 Nancy Carpenter.

Cover art and interior art from *Girl Wonder: A Baseball Story in Nine Innings* by Deborah Hopkinson, Illustrated by Terry Widener. Reprinted with the permission of Atheneum Books for Young Readers, an imprint of Simon &

Schuster Children's Publishing Division from *Girl Wonder, A Baseball Story in Nine Innings* by Deborah Hopkinson, illustrated by Terry Widener. Text Copyright © 2001 Deborah Hopkinson. Illustrations copyright © 2001 Terry Widener.

Cover art and interior art from *Apples to Oregon: Being the (Slightly) True Narrative of How a Brave Pioneer Father Brought Apples, Peaches, Pears, Plums, Grapes, and Cherries (And Children) Across the Plains* by Deborah Hopkinson, Illustrated by Nancy Carpenter. Reprinted with the permission of Atheneum Books for Young Readers, an imprint of Simon & Schuster Children's Publishing Division from *Apples to Oregon: Being the (Slightly) True Narrative of How a Brave Pioneer Father Brought Apples, Peaches, Pears, Plums, Grapes, and Cherries (And Children) Across the Plains* by Deborah Hopkinson, illustrated by Nancy Carpenter. Text Copyright © 2004 Deborah Hopkinson. Illustrations copyright © 2004 Nancy Carpenter.

Saving Strawberry Farm. Jacket art © 2005 by Rachel Isadora Turner. Used by permission of HarperCollins Publishers.

Sky Boys: How They Built the Empire State Building. Jacket art © 2006 by James Ransome, written by Deborah Hopkinson. Used by permission of Schwartz & Wade Books, an imprint of Random House, Inc.

Sweet Land of Liberty. Jacket Art © 2007 by Leonard Jenkins, written by Deborah Hopkinson. Used by permission of Peachtree Publishers.

Cover art and interior art from *The Prairie Skies Series – Book One: Pioneer Summer* by Deborah Hopkinson, Illustrated by Patrick Faricy. Reprinted with the permission of Aladdin Paperbacks, an imprint of Simon & Schuster Children's Publishing Division from *The Prairie Skies Series – Book One: Pioneer Summer* by Deborah Hopkinson, illustrated by Patrick Faricy. Text Copyright © 2002 Deborah Hopkinson. Illustrations copyright © 2002 Patrick Faricy.

Cover art and interior art from *The Prairie Skies Series – Book Two: Cabin in the Snow* by Deborah Hopkinson, Illustrated by Patrick Faricy. Reprinted with the permission of Aladdin Paperbacks, an imprint of Simon & Schuster Children's Publishing Division from *The Prairie Skies Series – Book Two: Cabin in the Snow* by Deborah Hopkinson, illustrated by Patrick Faricy. Text Copyright © 2002 Deborah Hopkinson. Illustrations copyright © 2002 Patrick Faricy.

Cover art and interior art from *The Prairie Skies Series – Book Three: Our Kansas Home* by Deborah Hopkinson, Illustrated by Patrick Faricy. Reprinted with the permission of Aladdin Paperbacks, an imprint of Simon & Schuster Children's Publishing Division from *The Prairie Skies Series – Book Three: Our Kansas Home* by Deborah Hopkinson, illustrated by Patrick Faricy. Text Copyright © 2003 Deborah Hopkinson. Illustrations copyright © 2003 Patrick Faricy.

Cover art and interior art from *The Klondike Kid Series – Book One: Sailing for Gold* by Deborah Hopkinson, Illustrated by Bill Farnsworth. Reprinted with the permission of Aladdin Paperbacks, an imprint of Simon & Schuster Children's Publishing Division from *The Klondike Kid Series – Book One: Sailing for Gold* by Deborah Hopkinson, illustrated by Bill Farnsworth. Text Copyright © 2004 Deborah Hopkinson. Illustrations copyright © 2004 Bill Farnsworth.

Cover art and interior art from *The Klondike Kid Series – Book Two: The Long Trail* by Deborah Hopkinson, Illustrated by Bill Farnsworth. Reprinted with the permission of Aladdin Paperbacks, an imprint of Simon & Schuster Children's Publishing Division from *The Klondike Kid Series – Book Two: The Long Trail* by Deborah Hopkinson, illustrated by Bill Farnsworth. Text Copyright © 2004 Deborah Hopkinson. Illustrations copyright © 2004 Bill Farnsworth.

Cover art and interior art from *The Klondike Kid Series – Book Three: Adventure in Gold Town* by Deborah Hopkinson, Illustrated by Bill Farnsworth. Reprinted with the permission of Aladdin Paperbacks, an imprint of Simon & Schuster Children's Publishing Division from *The Klondike Kid Series – Book Three: Adventure in Gold Town* by Deborah Hopkinson, illustrated by Bill Farnsworth. Text Copyright © 2004 Deborah Hopkinson. Illustrations copyright © 2004 Bill Farnsworth.

Cover of *Dear America, Hear My Sorrow: The Diary of Angela Denoto, A Shirtwaist Worker, 1909* by Deborah Hopkinson, 2004, reprinted by permission of Scholastic, Inc.

Cover of *Into the Firestorm: A Novel of San Francisco, 1906* by Deborah Hopkinson, reprinted by permission of Alfred A. Knopft, Inc., an imprint of Random House, Inc.

CHAPTER SEVEN

Cover of *Shutting Out the Sky: Life in the Tenements of New York, 1880–1924* by Deborah Hopkinson, 2004, reprinted by permission of Scholastic, Inc.

Cover of *Up Before Daybreak: Cotton and People in America,* by Deborah Hopkinson, 2006, reprinted by permission of Scholastic Nonfiction.

Photo of Boott Cotton Mills Museum by Deborah Hopkinson. Reprinted with permission.

Bluebird Summer. Jacket art © 2001 by Bethanne Andersen. Used by permission of HarperCollins Publishers.

A Packet of Seeds Jacket art © 2004 by Bethanne Andersen. Used by permission of HarperCollins Publishers.

Cover art and interior art from *Stories of Famous Americans: John Adams Speaks for Freedom* by Deborah Hopkinson, Illustrated by Craig Orback. Reprinted with the permission of Aladdin Paperbacks, an imprint of Simon & Schuster Children's Publishing Division from *Stories of Famous Americans: John Adams Speaks for Freedom* by Deborah Hopkinson, illustrated by Craig Orback. Text Copyright © 2005 Deborah Hopkinson. Illustrations copyright © 2005 Craig Orback.

Cover art and interior art from *Stories of Famous Americans: Susan B. Anthony: Fighter for Women's Rights* by Deborah Hopkinson, Illustrated by Amy Bates. Reprinted with the permission of Aladdin Paperbacks, an imprint of Simon & Schuster Children's Publishing Division from *Stories of Famous Americans: Susan B. Anthony: Fighter for Women's Rights* by Deborah Hopkinson, illustrated by Amy Bates. Text Copyright © 2005 Deborah Hopkinson. Illustrations copyright © 2005 Amy Bates.

Cover of *Who Was Charles Darwin?* Written by Deborah Hopkinson, Illustrated by Nancy Harrison © 2005. Reprinted with permission of Grosset and Dunlap.

Index

A Band of Angels 19–20, 23, 28, 44–45
A Packet of Seeds 80–82
Adams, Abigail 83
Adams, John 83–84, 88
Adventure in Gold Town 62, 64–66
Anderson, Bethanne 79–80
Anderson, Marian 55
Anthony, Susan B. 85–85, 88
Apples to Oregon, Being the (Slightly) True Narrative of How A Brave Pioneer Father Brought Apples, Peaches, Pears, Plums, Grapes, and Cherries (and Children) Across the Plains 50–51

Bates, Amy 84
Billy and the Rebel 23, 35–36
Birdie's Lighthouse 41–42
Bluebird Summer 79–80, 82

Cabin in the Snow 58–61
Carpenter, Nancy 46–47, 50–51
Chapman, Oscar 55
Civil War 23, 31–32, 35–36, 38–39, 59, 76
Colon, Raul 44

Darwin, Charles 86–88
Dear America: Hear My Sorrow, The Diary of Angela Denoto, A Shirtwaist Worker, New York City, 1909 67–68

Empire State Building 53–54

Fannie in the Kitchen 46–47
Faricy, Patrick 58–61
Farmer, Fannie Merritt 46–47
Farnsworth, Bill 62
Fisk University 23, 24–26, 44
Floca, Brian 35, 37–38
From Slave to Soldier 37

Gettysburg, Battle of 23, 25
Girl Wonder, A Baseball Story in Nine Innings 19, 48–49
Grant, Abigail Burgess 41–42

Harrison, Nancy 86
Historical fiction 17–26

Hopkinson, Deborah
 childhood 4–12
 children 12
 education 9, 11
 husband 12
 parents 4
 research process 21–22
 sisters 4
 writing career 15–16
 writing process 17–28
Hopkinson, Gloria 4–5
Hopkinson, Rebekah 7, 13, 15, 49
Hopkinson, Russell 4–5

Into the Firestorm, A Novel of San Francisco, 1906 69–70
Isadora, Rachel 52

Jenkins, Leonard 54
John Adams Speaks for Freedom 83–84

Kansas-Nebraska Act 59–61
Klondike Gold Rush 62–66, 71
Klondike Kid Series 62–66

Lanino, Deborah 42
Long Trail, The 62–66
Luelling, Henderson 50–51

Maria's Comet 19, 42–43
McCline, John 38–39
Mitchell, Maria 19, 43
Moore, Ella Sheppard 44

Orback, Craig 83
Our Kansas Home 58–61

Pioneer Summer 57–61
Prairie Skies Series 57–61

Ransome, James 31–34, 53
Research 21–22
Root, Kimberly Bulcken 41

Sailing for Gold 62, 64–66
San Francisco Fire and Earthquake 70–71

Saving Strawberry Farm 52
Shutting out the Sky, Life in the Tenements of New York 1880–1924 73–75, 77
Sky Boys, How They Built the Empire State Building 53–55
Susan B. Anthony, Fighter for Women's Rights 84–86
Sweet Clara and the Freedom Quilt 15, 19, 31–32, 34
Sweet Land of Liberty 54–55

Thomas, Andrew 11, 12–13
Thomas, Dimitri 12–14

Triangle Waist Company Fire 68, 71

Under the Quilt of Night 31, 33–34
Underground Railroad 31–34, 39
Up Before Daybreak, Cotton and People in America 75–78

Weiss, Alta 22, 48–49
Who Was Charles Darwin? 86–88
Widener, Terry 48

About the Author

Deborah Hopkinson is the author of books, short fiction, and nonfiction. Her works include *Sweet Clara and the Freedom Quilt*, winner of the 1994 International Reading Association Award; A Band of Angels, an ALA Notable book which also won the Golden Kite Award and was a Jane Addams Award Honor book; *Birdie's Lighthouse*, a Parents' Choice Silver Honor book, *Under the Quilt of Night*, winner of the Washington State Book Award, *Apples to Oregon*, winner of the Golden Kite Award and Spur Storytelling Award, and *Sky Boys: How They Built the Empire State Building*, winner of a *Boston Globe*-Horn Book Honor Award. Her nonfiction title, *Shutting Out the Sky: Life in the Tenements of New York 1880–1924*, was an honor book for the NCTE Orbis Pictus Award, a Jane Addams Award Honor book, an IRA Teacher's Choice, and a James Madison Award Honor book.

Born in Lowell, Massachusetts, Hopkinson holds a bachelor's degree in English at the University of Massachusetts and a master's degree in Asian Studies from the University of Hawai'i at Manoa. She and her husband, Andrew Thomas, are the parents of two grown children, Rebekah and Dimitri. Deborah Hopkinson lives in Corvallis, Oregon, where she serves as director of foundation relations for the Oregon State University Foundation.

For more information on Deborah Hopkinson's books as well as links to lesson plans and classroom activities, visit her Web site at www.deborahhopkinson.com. Contact information is available on the author's Web site.

www.ingramcontent.com/pod-product-compliance
Lightning Source LLC
Chambersburg PA
CBHW080940300426
44115CB00017B/2896